VARIETIES OF RELIGION TODAY

Institute for Human Sciences Vienna
Lecture Series

CHARLES TAYLOR

VARIETIES OF RELIGION TODAY

William James
Revisited

HARVARD UNIVERSITY PRESS

CAMBRIDGE, MASSACHUSETTS

AND LONDON, ENGLAND

First Harvard University Press paperback edition, 2003

Second printing, 2003

Library of Congress Cataloging-in-Publication Data

Taylor, Charles, 1931–

Varieties of religion today : William James revisited / Charles Taylor.

p. cm. — (Institute for Human Sciences Vienna lecture series)

Includes bibliographical references and index.

ISBN 0-674-00760-3 (cloth)

ISBN 0-674-01253-4 (paper)

1. James, William, 1842–1910. Varieties of religious experience.

2. Experience (Religion)   3. Psychology, Religious.   4. Religion.   I. Title.

II. Institute for Human Sciences Vienna lecture series.

BL53.J363 T39 2002

291.4′ 2—dc21   2001039872

PREFACE

In the spring of 1999 I delivered a set of Gifford Lectures in Edinburgh. In them I attempted to come to grips with the question "What does it mean to call our age secular?" and to offer an account of how we got to be that way. I am still struggling with these issues.

As I prepared the lectures, it was obvious that William James's *Varieties of Religious Experience* was an essential source. But it wasn't until I began rereading it that I remembered, or perhaps noticed for the first time, that this too had been a series of Gifford Lectures, delivered in Edinburgh almost a century earlier. The sense I had of treading in the footsteps of this trail-blazing predecessor was enhanced by the powerful recurring impression, in passage after passage of James's work, that (style and topical references aside) it could have been written yesterday, as against almost a hundred years ago.

This nearness says something both about James and about where we have come in our society and culture a turn of the century later. The idea gradually dawned of trying to articulate some of this, that is, of saying something of what I wanted to say about the place of religion in our secular age, in the form of a conversation/confrontation with James. The idea would be to disengage the way in which he captures something essential of our present predicament, while doing justice to the ways in which his take on religion could perhaps be considered too narrow and restrictive. This would have remained one of those intriguing thoughts that resonate semiarticulately in the back of one's mind, had not the Institute for Human Sciences in Vienna invited me to give a series of lectures in the spring of 2000, marking the centenary of Hans Gadamer's birth.

So I made this Vienna series the occasion for working out my exchange with James, the result of which is this book. This exchange is idiosyncratic and selective. *Varieties* is an immensely rich and multifaceted book. James has tremendously interesting things to say about a host of issues, including the psychology of religious belief, conversion, saintliness, mysticism, and the unconscious, which I leave to one side. I am approaching his book with a very specific agenda, asking what it can tell us about the place of religion today. In my argument I also draw on some of the essays published in *The Will to Believe.* I hope the narrowness of the focus does not obscure the eerie sense that so many of his readers have felt, that this long-dead author is in striking ways a contemporary.

CONTENTS

VARIETIES OF RELIGION TODAY

1

JAMES:
VARIETIES

1

It's almost a hundred years since William James delivered his celebrated Gifford Lectures in Edinburgh on *The Varieties of Religious Experience.*[1] I want in these pages to look again at this remarkable book, reflecting on what it has to say to us at the turn of a new century.

In fact it turns out to have a lot to say. It is astonishing how little dated it is. Some of the detail may be strange, but you easily think of examples in our world that fit the themes James is developing. You can even find yourself forgetting that these lectures were delivered a hundred years ago.

Which is not to say that there aren't questions one can raise about the way in which James conceives his subject. On the contrary; but this is not so much because of the difference between his time and ours; rather, these questions arise out of different ways of understanding religion that confronted each other then, and still do. To put it slightly more polemically: one could argue that James has certain blind spots in his view of religion. But these blind spots are widespread in the modern world. They are just as operative in our age as in his.

I want first to discuss these limitations in James's concept of religious experience. Then I will try to engage what moved him in this whole domain, which is the issue of the "twice-born," the center of religious experience that you feel throbbing not only in the lives that James writes about, but also in his own life. Finally, I make a few reflections on religion today, in relation to James's discussion.

WHAT IS RELIGIOUS EXPERIENCE?

People have pointed out the relative narrowness of the Jamesian perspective before. James sees religion primarily as something that individuals experience. He makes a distinction between living religious experience, which is that of the individual, and religious life, which is derivative because it is taken over from a community or church. For James, "your ordinary religious believer, who follows the conventional observances of his country," has a religion that "has been made for him by others . . . It would profit us little to study this second-hand religious life. We must make search rather for the original experiences which were the pattern-setters to all this mass of suggested feeling and imitated conduct. These experiences we can find only in individuals for whom religion exists not as a dull habit, but as an acute fever rather. But such individuals are 'geniuses' in the religious line" (6).

We see here the Jamesian view of religious life, its origins and continuance: there are people who have an original, powerful religious experience, which then gets communicated through some kind of institution; it gets handed on to others, and they tend to live it in a kind of secondhand way. In the transmission, the force and intensity of the original tends to get lost, until all that remains is "dull habit."

Later on, also toward the beginning of the book, James attempts to define religion as "the feelings, acts and experiences of individual men in their solitude, so far as they apprehend themselves to stand in relation to whatever they may consider the divine" (31). This is what is primary; it is out of religion in this sense that "theologies, philosophies and ecclesiastical organizations may secondarily grow." So churches play at best a secondary role, in transmitting and communicating the original inspiration.

I say "at best," because their effect can also be highly negative, stifling and distorting personal faith. James is not enamored of churches:

The word "religion" as ordinarily used, is equivocal. A survey of history shows us that, as a rule, religious geniuses attract disciples, and produce groups of sympathizers. When these groups get strong enough to "organize" themselves, they become ecclesiastical institutions with corporate ambitions of their own. The spirit of politics and the lust of dogmatic rule are then apt to enter and to contaminate the originally innocent thing; so that when we hear the word "religion" nowadays, we think inevitably of some "church" or other; and to some persons the word "church" suggests so much hypocrisy and tyranny and meanness and tenacity of superstition that in a wholesale undiscerning way they glory in saying that they are "down" on religion altogether. (334–335)

No wonder that "first-hand religious experience . . . has always appeared as a heretical sort of innovation." So that "when a religion has become an orthodoxy, its days of inwardness are over; the spring is dry; the faithful live at second hand exclusively and stone the prophets in their turn. The new church . . . can be henceforth counted as a staunch ally in every attempt to stifle the spontaneous religious spirit, and to stop all the later bubblings of the fountain from which in purer days it drew its own supply of inspiration" (337).

People who are against "religion," therefore, are often mistaken in their target. "The basenesses so commonly charged to religion's account are thus, almost all of them, not chargeable to religion proper, but rather to religion's wicked practical partner, the spirit of corporate dominion. And the bigotries are most of them in their turn chargeable to religion's wicked intellectual partner, the spirit of dogmatic dominion."

So the *real* locus of religion is in individual experience, and not in corporate life. That is one facet of the Jamesian thesis. But the other is that the real locus is in *experience,* that is, in feeling, as against the formulations by which people define, justify, rationalize their feelings (operations that are, of course, frequently undertaken by churches).

These two are clearly connected in James's mind. Feelings occur, he holds, in individuals; and in turn "individuality is founded in feeling" (501). The importance of feeling explains "why I have been so individualistic throughout these lectures." Now "compared with this world of living individualized feelings, the world of generalized objects which the intellect contemplates is without solidity or life" (502). Part of what gives feelings their primacy is that they determine conduct. One's feelings make a difference to one's action, a crucial point to a "pragmatist." But don't ideas as well? James thinks they don't, or not all to the same degree. Feelings generally determine conduct, without being inflected by the rationalizations. We can find a great variety of cases in which feeling and conduct are the same, while theories differ.

The theories which Religion generates, being thus variable, are secondary; and if you wish to grasp her essence, you must look to the feelings and the conduct as being the more constant elements. It is between these two elements that the short circuit exists on which she carries on her principal business, while the ideas and symbols and other institutions form loop-lines which may be perfections and improvements, and may even some day all be united into one harmonious system, but which are not to be regarded as organs with an indispensable function, necessary at all times for religion to go on. (504)

Now one can certainly criticize this take on religion. But before doing so, I should like to try to place it; that is, trace its origins and its place in our history and culture. It should be clear that this take is very much at home in modern culture.

We can trace its origins through a series of developments in our history. First, the emphasis on religion as personal is consonant with a major direction of change through the last several centuries in Latin Christendom. From the high Middle Ages, we can see a steadily increasing emphasis on a religion of personal commitment and devotion over forms centered on collective ritual. We can see this both in devotional movements and associations, like the Brethren of the Common Life in the fifteenth century, and in the demands made by church hierarchies and leaders on their members. An early example of the latter is the decision of the Lateran Council in 1215 to require all the faithful to confess to a priest and be shriven, so as to receive communion at least once a year.

From that point on, the pressure to adopt a more personal, committed, inward form of religion continued, through the preaching of the mendicant friars and others, through the devotional movements mentioned above, reaching a new stage with the Reformation. The point of declaring that salvation comes through faith was radically to devalue ritual and external practice in favor of inward adherence to Christ as Savior. It was not just that external ritual was of no effect, but that relying on it was tantamount to a presumption that we could control God. The Reformation also tended to delegitimate the distinction between fully committed believers and other, less devoted ones. As against a view of the church in which people operating at many different "speeds" coexisted, with religious "virtuosi," to use Max Weber's term, on one end, and ordinary intermittent practitioners on the other, all Christians were expected to be fully committed.

But this movement toward the personal, committed, inward didn't exist only in the Protestant churches. There was a parallel development in the Counter-Reformation, with the spread of different devotional movements, and the attempts to regulate the lives of the laity according to more and more stringent models of practice. The clergy were reformed, their training was upgraded; they were expected in turn to reach out and demand a higher level of personal practice from their flocks. A striking figure illustrates this whole movement: in the history of Catholic France, the moment at which the level of practice, as measured by baptisms and Easter communions, reaches its highest has been estimated to fall around 1870.[2] This was well after the anticlericalism of the Revolution and its attempts at dechristianization, and after a definite movement toward unbelief had set in among the educated classes. In spite of this incipient loss, the apogee of practice came this late because it stood at the end of a long process in which ordinary believers had been preached at, organized, sometimes bullied, into patterns of practice that reflected more personal commitment.

They had been pressed, we might be tempted to say, into "taking their religion seriously"; and this expression reflects how much James's take on religion, at least in one facet, is in line with our modern understanding. To take my religion seriously is to take it personally, more devotionally, inwardly, more committedly. Just taking part in external rituals, those that don't require the kind of personal engagement which, say, auricular confession, with its self-examination and promises of amendment, entails, is devalued on this understanding. This isn't what religion is really about.

This kind of understanding has deep roots, of course, in our religious tradition. When the psalmist, speaking for God, tells us to set aside our offerings of bulls and sheep and to offer instead a contrite heart (e.g., Psalm 51), we are already on the road to our contemporary notion of personal religion. But there were many stages along the way, and not every culture has pressed as singlemindedly toward this ultimate point as that of the Latin Christendom to which we are heirs in the West. There are other religious traditions in which devotional movements are important and admired, such as Hinduism with its modes of *bhakti,* but in which this devaluing of the life of collective ritual hasn't taken place. And there were earlier phases of our history in which the relation between those who were more personally devout and committed, and those whose main participation was in collective ritual, was thought of in terms of complementarity rather than ranked as more and less real; in which these two facets were understood to complete each other, be it in the life of an individual or in the religious life of the community. Moreover, there are certainly parts of the Catholic world where this is true today; only they tend to be distant from the North Atlantic regions, where the movement toward committed inwardness has gone the farthest.

In these regions, James's stress on personal religion, even his insistence that this is what religion *really* is, as

against collective practice, can seem entirely understandable, even axiomatic, to lots of people.

Indeed, this is so central to Western modernity that
a variant of this take is shared by highly secular people. It may take the form of their devaluing religion,
because they think it is inseparable from mindless or
unreflective external conformity; in other words, because they think that a really inward commitment
would have to free us from religion. That is exactly
what James fears and is trying to argue against in the
passage quoted above where he warns us against
defining "religion" in terms of "church," and thereby
dismissing it too quickly, and missing the value of the
real thing.

In fact, a striking feature of the Western march toward secularity is that it has been interwoven from the
start with this drive toward personal religion, as has
frequently been remarked.[3] The connections are mul-
tiple. It is not just that the falling off of religious belief
and practice has forced a greater degree of reflection
and commitment on those who remain. This has perhaps been evident in more recent times. It is much
more that the drive to personal religion has itself been
part of the impetus toward different facets of secular-

ization. It was this drive, for instance, which powerfully contributed to the disenchantment of the world of spirits and higher forces in which our ancestors lived. The Reformation and Counter-Reformation repressed magical practices, and then those facets of traditional Christian sacramental ritual that they began to deem magical; for Calvinists this even included the Mass. Later, at the time of the early American republic, a separation of church and state was brought about, mainly to give space for, and avoid the contamination of, personal religion, which itself had been given a further impetus through the Great Awakening.

Later again, the same stress on inwardness and serious commitment gave strength to the view that one should break with a religion in some of whose tenets one had difficulty believing. There is an "ethics of belief,"[4] and it should drive us into religious unbelief if we find that the evidence points that way. Moreover, many of the secular moralities that have taken the place of religion place the same stress on inner commitment. We have only to think of the hold of various forms of Kantianism on secular ethics.

In this sense, James's take on religion is well adapted to a confrontation between religion and secular views. It can seem the ground on which this confrontation can take place which is most favorable to religion: it operates within common assumptions about the importance of personal commitment, and within these it presents religion in the most favorable light by defining it in terms of intense experience that can galvanize conduct. This is not an accident. James's discussion of religious experience was not unconnected with his own profound commitments in this area, however the stance of psychological observer he assumes in this book might mislead us. In a sense, it articulates his own resistance to the agnostic intellectual culture of his day. I shall return to this below.

James's position thus emerges from the main sweep of Latin Christendom over recent centuries. But we still have to place it more exactly than that, because it clearly belongs to some rather than others of the subbranches that this development has thrown up. I want to relate it here to some of these crucial branching points.

There are modes of devotion in which we try to come closer to God, or center our lives on him, where we proceed in a fashion that trusts and builds on our own inner élan, our own desire to approach God. We see examples, on the Catholic side, in some of the major figures in what Henri Bremond has called "l'humanisme dévot" in the French seventeenth century, such as St. François de Sales;[5] or in Jesuit spirituality, which follows the inner guidance of consolation and desolation. On the Protestant side, we have the Cambridge Platonists, for instance, or Wesley (who himself was influenced by French Catholic spirituality).

This can be contrasted with a religious practice that stresses the demands made by God on his "unprofitable servants," which consists in following the Law, or God's commands, as these are prescribed in the tradition or Revelation, without necessarily relying for guidance on one's own inner sense of these things. It should be clear that this kind of practice can be as personal, committed, and "inward" as the devotional one, and it has been very prominent in the development of modern personal religion.

Of course, nothing prevents these two from combining in one religious life. One might even claim that they ought ideally to complement each other. I myself certainly lean in this direction, if I may step for a minute beyond the role of neutral commentator. But the fact is that they have frequently been polarized, and opposed to each other. Thus, in the remarkable spiritual flourishing of the French seventeenth century, devout humanism was strongly opposed by thinkers of the Jansenist persuasion, like Arnault and Nicole.[6] One can understand why. The hyper-Augustinian sense of our own sinfulness, even depravity, which was central to Jansenus' message, made it seem not only dangerous but presumptuous to trust the élan toward God that one (believes one) finds within. And famously, the later years of the century saw the epic battle between Bossuet and Fénelon on this very issue: dare one aspire to an "amour pur" for God, or must one be actuated by fear of him?

We can perhaps see something of the same polarization in various periods of Islamic history, including today. There is a facet of Islamic practice that emphasizes full compliance with the *shar'ia,* and another that has been carried, for instance, by traditions of Sufism, and that build on the longing of the soul for unity with God, as in Rumi's famous image of the reed flute. These have often been united, but there have also been times in which the first stream has turned with suspicion on the second. The hostility to Sufism among some contemporary Islamist movements is a case in point.[7]

If we see this contrast as an important branching point between two streams, then plainly James stands in that of devout humanism. But we need to situate him more precisely within this line. He plainly belongs to that strand of it which is ready to challenge the traditionally mediated revelation in the name of one's inner inspiration. His model is more George Fox the Quaker than it is St. François de Sales. Indeed, he quotes Fox at length in the continuation of the passage I cited above (335–336).

We can situate him further in another branching: he sides with the religion of the heart over that of the head. This was plain in the passage I quoted above about the irrelevance of theories to real religious life. He stands in the succession of that late seventeenth- and eighteenth-century revolt against intellectualism in religion, following the Pietists and John Wesley in Christianity, the Hassidim in Judaism, which sees the fullness of religious commitment as lying in powerful emotions and their expression, rather than in the nuances of doctrine or the perfections of scholarship.

Now this whole stream of devout humanism, in its anarchic and emotive branches, passed through a number of transpositions en route to James in the late nineteenth century. One of these was Romanticism, wherein the inspired initiator of a new inward spirituality is thought of as the "genius"—a term that figured in my earlier quote about the "pattern-setters" of religion (6). And along with this comes the notion that the genius cannot really be fully followed by ordinary people. The full intensity of the experience is always to some extent blunted as the pattern of spirituality comes to be adopted by large groups. The intense heat of the original feeling cools; what was "acute fever" becomes "dull habit."

We are reminded of the contemporary theological teaching of Harnack in Germany, who depicted the white-hot charisma of the New Testament period as cooling into routine under the constraints of institutionalization. This whole understanding of moral/spiritual life, in which routinization of inspiration is understood as a quasi-inevitable fate, like entropy in the physical universe, was secularized and diffused by Weber, who even borrowed the New Testament term "charisma" from Harnack. Charismatic interventions in history suffer unavoidably from "banalization" ("Veralltäglichung," usually translated "routinization"). Weber even uses entropy as a master image here. Charisma is the specifically "revolutionary creative power of history," but all existing charismatic force is somewhere on its way "from the original storm to a slow death by suffocation."[8]

This picture of the interplay of inspiration and banalization, so widespread in the post-Romantic but secular world, also shapes the outlook of William James.

IN WHAT WAYS does this situation within these different branchings limit the scope of James's study? How are the phenomena of religion distorted or narrowed through being conceived in terms of religious "experience"?

Well, obviously, we can't expect too much fit with religious life that is far away from the modern North Atlantic norms, which put such an emphasis on personal religion. But it would be churlish, even absurd, to hold against him that his discussion didn't relate very closely to the practice of Hindus in contemporary India. That wasn't his main focus, which was really about religion as we know it on our culture (although there is the occasional reference outside, to, e.g., the Buddha and al-Ghazzali), a limitation that was quite understandable a century ago. In order to focus the discussion, I intend to follow James and concentrate on the North Atlantic world (although I, too, find it hard to resist the occasional glance sideways to other regions).

But one might counterattack and say that after all, he's talking about religious *experience;* he's not claiming anything about all the other forms that figure on the other branches I mentioned above, the ones he is not situated within. This answer, however, won't wash, because the issue is very much whether, in taking his stand where he does, he doesn't severely distort the other branches. And indeed, it is difficult to imagine not doing so. I have situated James in various branchings of our religious culture, and these branchings were the sites of vigorous polemic. A Fox, a Wesley didn't only take one branch; they condemned the other. Condemnations may of course be totally justified, but more often than not they are attended with some distortion; the question is, to what extent the ones that James falls heir to give him a mangled and partial view of some of the important phenomena of modern religious life.

Nothing is farther from my intention than to indulge in point-scoring here. The aim is not to show that James's sympathies were narrow. Indeed, exactly the opposite is the case. One of the things that make his book so remarkable is the wide sympathy, coupled with unparalleled phenomenological insight, which mark James as the exceptional figure that he is. That's why we go on reading this book, and will go on finding ideas of extraordinary value in it well after its centenary has passed. As to the unfortunate fact that James is neglected by contemporary academic philosophers, with a few honorable exceptions, this may just show that, alas, wide sympathy and powers of phenomenological description are not qualities for which the discipline has much place at present.

But in spite of all this, it seems to me that James got certain things wrong; or saw some important phenomena less undistortively than others. And any assessment of his work has to come to grips with this. The more so, in that just because of the close fit between James's take on religion and certain aspects of modern culture, one might easily run away with the idea that what James describes as religious experience is the only form religion can assume today. As we shall see below, especially in the third chapter, there are important developments that might make this appear so, but it is not so.

So what did James get wrong, or at least less right? One good place to start is with something that he sees himself: he stands within a Protestant tradition of understanding. So one thing he has trouble getting his mind around is Catholicism. His wide sympathies fail him, for instance, when it comes to St. Theresa of Avila. She is one of his sources, and he quotes her at length (408–410), but at another point he says in some exasperation that "in the main her idea of religion seems to have been that of an endless amatory flirtation—if one may say so without irreverence—between the devotee and the deity" (347–348).

More important, he has trouble getting beyond a certain individualism. Churches are necessary, he clearly concedes. How else can the set of insights around a certain intense experience be handed on? How else can others be inducted into them? How else can believers be organized to take the action that flows from their faith? Of course, something is inevitably lost as religion thus becomes "second-hand," but the alternative would be no transmission at all.

What doesn't figure here is the way what one might call the religious connection, the link between the believer and the divine (or whatever), may be essentially mediated by corporate, ecclesial life. Thus let us imagine taking up the other branch to which I contrasted devout humanism, so that we think of religion (also) as living out the demands made by God, or the ways we are called upon to follow by some higher source. Let us imagine further that these ways are in some respect inherently social: say, that we are called upon to live together in brotherly love, and to radiate outward such love as a community. Then the locus of the relation with God is (also) through the community, and not simply in the individual. But this is the way that the life of the Christian church has been conceived, among many Protestants as well as Catholics; and also the way Israel and the Islamic *umma* have been conceived. Moreover, this is far from being a thing of the past; this is still the way in which many today understand their religious life. What James can't seem to accommodate is the phenomenon of collective religious life, which is not just the result of (individual) religious connections, but which in some way constitutes or *is* that connection. In other words, he hasn't got place for a collective connection through a common way of being.

There is also another kind of collective connection, which is even farther off his map, perhaps because it is quintessentially "Catholic." This is the connection that consists in the fact that the church is a sacramental communion; some of the force is carried in an expression like "mystical body." From one point of view, this is just a facet of the connection through the church's common way of being. But it raises more explicitly the idea of God's life interpenetrating ours, and of this interpenetration being made fuller, more intense and immediate through our own practices. These practices cover the whole range, including those we might call ethical, or more generally the practices of charity; but the connection gains a certain intensity in the signs instituted to manifest it, which are called sacraments.

It goes without saying that this sacramental connection is also essentially collective; in fact it participates in the collective nature of the other kind of connection, which turns on a common way of life.

These kinds of things don't find a place in James's conceptual grid, and this fact partly accounts for the highly negative view about churches. Not that they aren't also full of the two "spirits of dominion" he cites. This is especially true of the Catholic church in Western Christendom, whose life in recent centuries has frequently been marred by a drive to dominate. But if a church is also a locus of collective connection, then one will not be able to think of it so exclusively in the negative terms that James displays.

A parallel point could be made about James's exclusion of theology from the center of religious life. This is particularly difficult for Christianity to accommodate. Not that there hasn't frequently been over-theologization, in the sense of an insistence on fine distinctions, even to the point of splitting churches on these issues, where a greater sense of what is essential, less ego invested in one's formulations, and a more abundant charity, might have averted schism. But the devotional, practical, and (if any) sacramental way of life needs some minimum articulation of what it is all about: some propositional formulations are unavoidable—about God, creation, Christ, and the like. Just as the life can't be separated from its collective expression, so it can't be isolated from a minimum of express formulation. The faith, the hope are *in* something.

But here we push against the bounds of another criticism of James. Up to now, I've been pleading that there are important, widespread religious forms that cannot be undistortively understood within his concept of religious experience. This is in a sense an empirical point. But one might make the more radical conceptual or transcendental point, that the very idea of an experience that is in no way formulated is impossible. The familiar arguments of Hegel (say, in the *Phenomenology of Spirit,* chapter 1), or of Wittgenstein (say, in the *Philosophical Investigations*, I @261) come to mind. The experience can have no content at all if you can't say *anything* about it.

Of course, James was well cognizant of Hegel, albeit resistant to being recruited into the neo-Hegelianism of his day. He would have seen the point of this objection, and carried on with the reply that having *some* description is not the same as being theorized, and particularly not the same as being authoritatively theorized by some official magisterium that can lean on you for the heterodoxy of your experience.

The point is well taken, but it ought to force us towards a more adequate account of the implicit distinction here between ordinary unavoidable description and theorizing. Where does one draw the line? More to the point: do certain "experiences"—St. Theresa's, for instance—require rather more in the way of propositional background than others? If there are some that require quite a lot, what becomes in such cases of the supposed short circuit whereby feeling bypasses theory on its way to influencing conduct?

A similar set of considerations might be deployed to question the sense in which one can really have an individual experience. All experiences require some vocabulary, and these are inevitably in large part handed

to us in the first place by our society, whatever trans-
formations we may ring on them later. The ideas, the
understanding with which we live our lives, shape directly what we could call religious experience; and
these languages, these vocabularies, are never those
simply of an individual.[9]

Does this make James's main thesis, about real religion being individual experience, unstatable? Not at
all. We can make the point in the terms I mentioned
above, where the question reposes on whether the religious connection is individual or collective. But once
we fully appreciate the social nature of language, it
does open another series of questions for James. There
are (what are in one sense) individual experiences that
are immensely enhanced by the sense that they are
shared. I am sitting at home watching the local hockey
team win the Stanley Cup. I rejoice in this. But the
sense of my joy here is framed by my understanding
that thousands of fans all over the city, some gathered
at the rinkside, others also in their living rooms, are
sharing in this moment of exultation. There are certain emotions you can have in solidarity that you can't
have alone; the experience mutates into something
else by the fact that it is shared. How much of what
James thinks of as individual experience is socially en-

hanced or affected in this way? We could imagine a sect in which the individual's relation to God is everything; and yet people are brought into contact with God through revival meetings. They come to conversion at that climactic moment of decision when the preacher calls on people to come forward and declare their faith. This can be a white-hot experience, but in what sense is it individual? There are a number of questions here that need to be resolved.[10]

All that I have said above is meant to try to situate James's focus in the map of modern religious phenomena. He doesn't cover the whole field, but his vision is proportionately more intense of the realities he does fix his gaze on. It is these that I want to turn to next.

2

THE
"TWICE-BORN"

I want now to engage with the very heart of James's discussion, which I identify with the description of the plight of the "twice-born." Their contrast case, the "once-born," are healthy-minded. They have the sense that all is well with the world and/or that they are on the right side of God. After citing a number of cases, James comments: "one can but recognize in such writers . . . the presence of a temperament organically weighted on the side of cheer and fatally forbidden to linger, as those of the opposite temperament linger, over the darker aspects of the universe" (83).

As against these, there are the "sick souls," who cannot help but see the pain, the loss, the evil, the suffering in the world. Of course, a typically Jamesian playfulness and irony is running through these passages. Once a distinction is made with a contrasting classification like "healthy" and "sick," it would seem axiomatic that the former is to be preferred. But in fact James stands on the other side; he identifies with the sick here. Not just that this is where he classes himself, without, of course, explicitly saying so. (Research has shown that one of the examples he quotes of deep metaphysical depression, attributed to a "Frenchman," actually describes his own earlier experience.) But also in that he sees the sick as being more profound and insightful here.

As he moves from describing the healthy-minded "to the unpleasant task of hearing what the sick souls . . . have to say of the secrets of their prison-house, their own peculiar form of consciousness," he declares: "Let us then resolutely turn our backs on the once-born and their sky-blue optimistic gospel; let us not simply cry out, in spite of all appearances, 'Hurrah for the Universe!—God's in his Heaven, all's right with the world.' Let us see rather whether pity, pain, and fear, and the sentiment of human helplessness may not open a profounder view and put into our hands a more complicated key to the meaning of the situation" (135–136).

What do the sick souls see that their healthy cousins don't? We might summarize that they see the abyss over which we stand. But as we follow James's discussion, we can distinguish three forms that this consciousness can take.

The first might be called religious melancholy. "The world now looks remote, strange, sinister, uncanny."

Things seem unreal, distant, as though seen through a cloud (151–152). Another way of putting this would be to speak of a loss of meaning. In describing Tolstoy's experience, James says of him that "the sense that life had any meaning whatever was for a time wholly withdrawn" (151).

The second, which James also calls "melancholy," is characterized by fear. The intentional object here is the world not so much as meaningless, but rather as evil. And as we get to the more severe forms, what threatens is "desperation absolute and complete, the whole universe coagulating about the sufferer into a material of overwhelming horror, surrounding him without opening or end. Not the conception or intellectual perception of evil, but the grisly blood-freezing heart-palsying sensation of it close upon one . . . Here is the real core of the religious problem: Help! Help!" (162). (This is incidentally the form of melancholy experienced by James's "Frenchman" [160–161]).

The third form of the abyss is the acute sense of personal sin. Here he is talking about, for example, people reacting to standard Protestant revival preaching and feeling a terrible sense of their own sinfulness, even being paralyzed by it—perhaps to be later swept up into the sense of being saved.

James speaks again here of the superiority of the "morbid-minded" view. The normal process of life contains many things to which melancholy (of the second kind, the fear of evil) is the appropriate response: the slaughterhouse, death.

Crocodiles and rattlesnakes and pythons are at this moment vessels of life as we are; their loathsome existence fills every minute of every day that drags its length along; and whenever they or other wild beasts clutch their living prey, the deadly horror which an agitated melancholiac feels is literally the right reaction to the situation. (163–164)

The completest religions would therefore seem to be those in which the pessimistic elements are best developed. Buddhism, of course, and Christianity are the best known to us. They are essentially religions of deliverance: the man must die to an unreal life before he can be born into the real life. (165)

Those who have been through this kind of thing and come out on the other side are the "twice-born." Just as religious experience is the more authentic reality of religion, so this experience is the deeper and more truly religious one. It is thus at the heart of religion properly understood. It is an experience of deliverance. It yields a "state of assurance," of salvation, or the meaningfulness of things, or the ultimate triumph of goodness. Its fruits are a "loss of all worry, the sense that all is ultimately well with one, the peace, the harmony, the *willingness to be*, even though the outer conditions should remain the same" (248). The world appears beautiful and more real, in contrast to the "dreadful unreality and strangeness" felt in melancholy. We are also empowered; the inhibitions and divisions that held us back melt away in the condition James calls "Saintliness" (271). It gives us a sense of being connected to a wider life and a greater power, a sense of elation and freedom, "as the outlines of confining selfhood melt down," a "shifting of the emotional centre towards loving and harmonious affections" (272–273).

This is at the heart of religion for James, because this experience meets our most dire spiritual needs, which are defined by the three great negative experiences of melancholy, evil, and the sense of personal sin. Some of the perennial interest of James's book comes from his identifying these three zones of spiritual anguish, which continue to haunt our world today.

The third one, the sense of personal sin, may be less

common among James's readers, who generally belong to the educated classes, which are disproportion-
ately nonbelievers and, when they have some faith
commitment, are unlikely to find it in those modes of
evangelical Protestantism in which this sense is the
most acute. And yet who can fail to notice that this
kind of religion, and the experience of personal evil
and deliverance which it makes central, is alive and in
full expansion in our day. This is not true only in the
United States, but even more so in Latin America, Africa, and even in parts of Asia. Some have estimated
that evangelical Christianity is the fastest-growing
form of religious life, faster than or as fast as Islam—
but this is the more remarkable in that its expansion
is largely the result of conversion, whereas Islam's
comes mainly from natural growth.[1]

The surge of evangelical Protestantism often occurs
in contexts where community has broken down, in
Third World countries, where people have been
pitched into urban life, often in chaotic circumstances
and without support systems. They can be over-
whelmed by a sense of personal incapacity or evil, but
find that they can overcome crippling failings and
weaknesses, drink or drugs or drifting or whatever, by

surrendering themselves in a conversion experience. It would appear that entering the Nation of Islam has wrought a similar change in the lives of some African-Americans. Here is a very important religious phenomenon, whose incidence seems to be growing with developing modernity and which figures in James's account.

Melancholy is, of course, a phenomenon long recognized. It goes back well into the premodern world. But its meaning has changed. The sudden sense of the loss of significance, which is central to melancholy, or accidie or ennui, used to be experienced in a framework in which the meaning of things was beyond doubt. God was there, good and evil were defined, what we are called to cannot be gainsaid; but we can no longer feel it. We are suddenly on the outside, exiled. Accidie is a sin, a kind of self-exclusion, for which there can be no justification.

But in the modern context, melancholy arises in a world where the guarantee of meaning has gone, where all its traditional sources, theological, metaphysical, historical, can be cast in doubt. It therefore has a new shape: not the sense of rejection and exile from an unchallengeable cosmos of significance, but rather the intimation of what may be a definitive emptiness, the final dawning of the end of the last illusion of significance. It hurts, one might say, in a new way.

One might argue which mode of melancholy hurts more: my exile from the general feast of meaning, or the threatened implosion of meaning altogether. But there is no doubt which has the greater significance. The first pain touches me, the second everyone and everything.

The shift to the new mode and context of melancholy is clearly marked in the life and work of Baudelaire. Against the background of a real cosmic significance which I am perversely incapable of rejoicing in, taking the side of evil seems pointless; but where the threat is the ground zero of all meaning, even the recovery of evil is a gain. Baudelaire's "spleen" poems accomplish a paradoxical liberation: in describing the empty world, the lowered, leaden sky, they lift its weight from my shoulders, by giving this burden a visage and a shape. The ground zero of melancholy has always been that one loses even the sense of what has been lost, even awareness of the source of the pain. To the extent that melancholy has a place in the cosmic order, as one of the "humours," which is in turn connected by "correspondences" to other realities, one can escape the ground zero by portraying its characteristic symbols, as Dürer does. But by the time of Baudelaire, where even the correspondences have to be reinvented, our only recourse is to paint the lack, the evil itself. Hence the new spiritual power of something that can be described as "les fleurs du mal."

Melancholy, modern style, in the form of a sense of perhaps ultimate meaninglessness, is the recognized modern threat. We readily see it as a danger that menaces all of us. We even see our philosophies and spiritual positions as addressed to this threat, as attempts to rebut or thwart a sense of meaninglessness. It is common to construe the history of religion through this prism, as though from the beginning we could see it as an answer to the inherent meaninglessness of things. This is a view implicit in Weber, I would argue, made more explicit in Gauchet.[2] I think this is a serious distortion, but there is obviously some truth in it. And once more, we see James identifying a crucial area of modern spiritual malaise.

But how about the third version of the abyss, the sense of enveloping evil? This is less widely recognized. Awareness of it can even be eclipsed by the sense that our great problem in a secular age, after the "death of God," is meaninglessness. The sense of evil seems to partake too much of the metaphysical dimension that we are supposed to have left behind us in modernity. But I believe that it defines just as important a threat, if not more urgent than the loss of meaning. As the sense of a guaranteed order in which good can triumph recedes, the sense of the surrounding evil, within us and without, which James so well describes, faces no obvious defenses. It cannot but deeply disturb us. Indeed, one can suspect that we sometimes take flight into the meaninglessness of things in order to avoid facing it, just as Baudelaire in a sense moved in the opposite direction, while aestheticizing evil to make it bearable. But beyond that, the fierce, often violent, moralism of the modern age constitutes one of our most important defenses against this sense of pervasive evil.

If even some of this is true, we can once more credit James with an extraordinary insight into the spiritual needs of the modern world.

WHAT WAS JAMES'S TAKE on religion doing for James? Or, put more impersonally, what was the wider agenda of which it was part? I believe it was a crucial part of James's argument, with himself and his contemporaries, about the admissibility of belief. It was an important part of his *apologia pro fide sua.*)

Like any sensitive intellectual of his time and place, (James had to argue against the voices, within and without, that held that religion was a thing of the past, that one could no longer in conscience believe in this kind of thing in an age of science.) Already a passage in *Varieties* gives a sense of what is at stake in this inner debate. James is speaking of those who are for one reason or another incapable of religious conversion. He refers to some whose "inaptitude" is intellectual in origin:

Their religious faculties may be checked in their natural tendency to expand, by beliefs about the world that are inhibitive, the pessimistic and materialistic beliefs, for example, within which so many good souls, who in former times would have freely indulged their religious propensities, find themselves nowadays, as it were, frozen; or the agnostic vetoes upon faith as something weak and shameful, under which so many of us to-day lie cowering, afraid to use our instincts. (204)

But a fuller discussion of these "agnostic vetoes," and the answer to them, occurs in "The Will to Believe."[3] Here it is plain that the main source of the vetoes is a kind of ethics of belief (and William Clifford's work is explicitly cited, e.g., WB 17–18). Clifford's view in *The Ethics of Belief* starts from a notion of what proper scientific procedure is: never turn your hypotheses into accepted theories until the evidence is adequate. It then promotes this into a moral precept for life in general. The underlying picture of our condition is that we find certain hypotheses more pleasing, more flattering, more comforting, and are thus tempted to believe them. It is the path of manliness, courage, and integrity to turn our backs on these facile comforts, and face the universe as it really is. But so strong are the temptations to deviate from this path that we must make it an unbreakable precept never to give our assent unless the evidence compels it.

With his unrivaled gift for striking rhetoric mixed with irony and gentle, over-the-top parody, James evokes this view:

When one turns to the magnificent edifice of the physical sciences, and sees how it was reared; what thousands of disinterested moral lives of men lie buried in its mere foundations; what patience and postponement, what choking down of preferences, what submission to the icy laws of outer fact are wrought into its very stones and mortar; how absolutely impersonal it stands in its vast augustness—then how besotted and contemptible seems every little sentimentalist who comes blowing his voluntary smoke-wreaths, and pretending to decide things from out of his private dream! (WB 17)

On the same page James quotes Clifford: "Belief is desecrated when given to unproved and unquestioned statements, for the solace and private pleasure of the believer . . . Whoso would deserve well of his fellows in this matter will guard the purity of his belief with a very fanaticism of jealous care, lest at any time it should rest on an unworthy object, and catch a stain which can never be wiped away." The pleasure of illicit belief is a stolen one, asserts Clifford. "It is sinful, because it is stolen in defiance of our duty to mankind. That duty is to guard ourselves from such beliefs as from a pestilence, which may shortly master our own body and then spread to the rest of the town . . . It is wrong always, and everywhere, and for anyone, to believe anything upon insufficient evidence" (WB 17–18: One wonders who is more over the top?).

James opposes to this his own counterprinciple:

The thesis I defend is, briefly stated, this: Our passional nature not only lawfully may, but must, decide an option between propositions, whenever it is a genuine option that cannot by its nature be decided on intellectual grounds; for to say, under such circumstances, "Do not decide, but leave the question open," is itself a passional decision—just like deciding yes or no—and is attended with the same risk of losing the truth. (WB 20)

Backing this principle is his own view of the human predicament. Clifford assumes that there is only one road to truth: we put the hypotheses that appeal to us under severe tests, and those that survive are worthy of adoption—the kind of procedure whose spirit was recaptured in our time by Popper's method of conjectures and refutation. To put it dramatically, we can win the right to believe a hypothesis only by first treating it with maximum suspicion and hostility.

James holds, on the contrary, that there are some domains in which truths will be hidden from us unless we go at least halfway toward them. Do you like me or not? If I am determined to test this by adopting a stance of maximum distance and suspicion, the chances are that I will forfeit the chance of a positive answer. An analogous phenomenon on the scale of the whole society is social trust; doubt it root and branch, and you will destroy it.

Here are, then, cases, where a fact cannot come at all unless a preliminary faith exists in its coming. *And where faith in a fact can help create the fact,* that would be an insane logic which should say that faith running ahead of scientific evidence is the "lowest kind of immorality" into which a thinking being can fall. (WB 28–29)

But can the same kind of logic apply to religion, that is, to a belief in something that by hypothesis is way beyond our power to create? James thinks it can. What is created is not God or the eternal,[4] but there is a certain grasp of these, and a certain succor from these that can never be ours unless we open ourselves to them in faith. James is, in a sense, building on the Augustinian insight that in certain domains love and self-opening enable us to understand what we would never grasp otherwise, rather than just following on understanding as its normal consequence.[5]

What does that tell us about what the path of rationality consists in for someone who stands on the threshold, deciding whether he should permit himself to believe in God? On one side is the fear of believing something false if he follows his instincts here. But on the other there is the hope of opening out what are now inaccessible truths through the prior step of faith.

Faced with this double possibility it is no longer so clear that Clifford's ethic is the appropriate one, because it was taking account of only the first possibility. The two possibilities define an option, and indeed a forced one, in that there is no third way: to suspend judgement is just as surely to forgo the hope of new truth as to judge negatively.

So Clifford's principle has to be rephrased as a choice: *"Better risk loss of truth than chance of error—* that is your faith-vetoer's exact position" (WB 30). But in what does this demonstrate superior rationality to the contrary option?

To preach skepticism to us as a duty until "sufficient evidence" for religion be found, is tantamount therefore to telling us, when in the presence of the religious hypothesis, that to yield to our fear of its being error is wiser and better than to yield to our hope that it may be true. It is not intellect against all passions, then; it is only one passion laying down its law. And by what, forsooth, is the supreme wisdom of this passion warranted? Dupery for dupery, what proof is there that dupery through hope is so much worse than dupery through fear? I, for one, can see no proof; and I simply refuse obedience to the scientist's command to imitate his kind of option, in a case where my own stake is important enough to give me the right to choose my own form of risk. (WB 30–31)

I, therefore, cannot see my way to accepting the agnostic rules for truth-seeking, or willfully agree to keep my willing nature out of the game. I cannot do so for the plain reason, that *a rule of thinking which would absolutely prevent me from acknowledging certain kinds of truth if those kinds of truth were really there, would be an irrational rule.* (WB 31–32)

The minimal form of James's argument is, then, that the supposed superior rationality of the "agnostic veto" on belief—don't believe in God until you have overwhelming evidence—disappears once you see that there is an option between two risks of loss of truth. Everybody should be free to choose his own kind of risk. But this minimal form easily flips into a stronger variant, which is captured by the italicized clause I have just quoted. Taking the agnostic stance could here be taxed as the less rational one.

This is for grounds similar to those laid out in Pascal's famous wager. James has already evoked this (WB 16–17) and treated it rather caustically. But on reflection, this may be because the Pascalian form is specifically directed to converting the interlocutor to Catholicism, to "masses and holy water." But if one takes the general form of Pascal's argument here—that you should weight two risks not only by their probabilities but also by their prospective "payoffs"—then James himself seems to entertain something of the sort. Religion is not only a "forced option," that is, one in which there is no third way, no way of avoiding choice, but it is also a *"momentous* option. We are supposed to gain, even now, by our belief, and to lose by our non-belief, a certain vital good" (WB 30).

The likeness increases when we reflect that Pascal never thought of his wager argument as standing alone, appealing as it were purely to the betting side of our nature, to the instincts that take over when we enter the casinos at Las Vegas. He, too, holds the Augustinian view that in matters divine we need to love before we know:

Et de là vient qu'au lieu qu'en parlant de choses humaines on dit qu'il faut les connaître avant de les aimer; ce qui a passé en proverbe, les saints au contraire disent en parlant de choses divines qu'il faut les aimer pour les connaître, et qu'on n'entre dans la verité que par la charité, don't ils ont fait une de leurs plus utiles sentences.[6]

But the issue could be put in other terms again. The single-risk view of the agnostics seems more plausible than James's double-risk thesis because they take for granted that our desires can only be an obstacle to our finding the truth. The crucial issue is thus the place of "our volitional nature" in the theoretical realm. The very idea that things will go better in the search for truth if you keep passion, desire, and willing out seems utterly implausible to James—not just for the reason he thinks he has demonstrated, that certain truths only open to us as a result of our commitment, but also because it seems so clear to him that we never operate this way.

So one way he frames the issue is that the agnostic vetoers are asking that he "wilfully agree to keep my willing nature out of the game." But from another standpoint, neither side is really doing this. Agnosticism "is not intellect against all passions, then; it is only intellect with one passion laying down its law" (WB 30–31). To put it in the harsh language of a later politics, those who claim to be keeping passion out are suffering from false consciousness. This is not the way the mind works at all.

This is the point he makes in a subsequent article in *The Will to Believe,* with the arresting title "Reflex Action and Theism" (WB 90–113, esp. 99–102). But we can return to *Varieties* and see the claim laid out there.

Rationalism gives an account of only a part of our mental life, and one that is "relatively superficial."

It is the part which has the *prestige* undoubtedly, for it has the loquacity, it can challenge you for proofs, and chop logic, and put you down with words. But it will fail to convince or convert you all the same, if your dumb intuitions are opposed to its conclusions. If you have intuitions at all, they come from a deeper level of your nature than the loquacious level which rationalism inhabits. Your whole subconscious life, your impulses, your faiths, your needs, your divinations, have prepared the premises, of which your consciousness now feels the weight of the result; and something in you absolutely *knows* that that result must be truer than any logic-chopping rationalistic talk, however clever, that may contradict it. (73)

James has in a sense opened up to view an important part of the struggle between belief and unbelief in modern culture. We can see it, after a fashion, from both sides of the fence: even though James has himself come down on one side, we can still feel the force of the other side. Of course, the objections to belief are not only on epistemological grounds. There are also those who feel that the God of theism has utterly failed the challenge of theodicy, how we can believe in a good and omnipotent God, given the state of the world. James addresses this question too, in another essay in *The Will to Believe* ("Is Life Worth Living?" WB 34–56).

But if we keep to the epistemological-moral issue of the ethics of belief, James clarifies why it always seems to end in a standoff. (1) Each side is drawing on very different sources, and (2) our culture as a whole cannot seem to get to a point where one of these no longer speaks to us. And yet (3) we cannot seem to function at all unless we relate to one or the other.

(1) The reason the argument is so difficult, and so hard to join, is that each side stands within its own view of the human moral predicament. The various facets of each stance support each other, so that there seems nowhere you can justifiably stand outside. The agnostic view propounds some picture (or range of pictures) of the universe and human nature. This has going for it that it can claim to result from "science," with all the prestige that this carries with it. It can even look from the inside as though this was all you need to say. But from the outside it isn't at all clear that what everyone could agree are the undoubted findings of

modern natural science quite add up to a proof of, say, materialism, or whatever the religion-excluding view is.

From the inside the "proof" seems solid, because certain interpretations are ruled out on the grounds that they seem "speculative" or "metaphysical." From the outside, this looks like a classical *petitio principii*. But from the inside the move seems unavoidable, because it is powered by certain ethical views. These are the ones that James laid bare: it is wrong, uncouraageous, unmanly, a kind of self-indulgent cheating, to have recourse to this kind of interpretation, which we know appeals to something in us, offers comfort, or meaning, and which we therefore should fend off, unless absolutely driven to them by the evidence, which is manifestly not the case. The position holds firm because it locks together a scientific-epistemological view and a moral one.

From the other side, the same basic phenomena show up, but in an entirely different shape. One of the crucial features that justify aversion to certain interpretations from the agnostic standpoint, namely that they in some way *attract* us, shows up from the believer's standpoint as what justifies our interest. And that very much for the reasons which James explores, namely that this attraction is the hint that there is something important here which we need to explore further, that this exploration can lead us to something of vital significance, which would otherwise remain closed to us. Epistemology and ethics (in the sense of intuitions about what is of crucial importance) combine here.

From this standpoint, the agnostic's closure is self-inflicted, the claim that there is nothing here which ought to interest us a kind of self-fulfilling prophecy. A similar accusation of circularity is hurled in the other direction. The believer is thought to have invented the delusion that beguiles him.

Each stance creates in a sense a total environment, in the sense that whatever considerations occur in one appear transformed in the other. They can't be appealed to in order to decide the issue, because as they pass from one stance to the other they bear a changed meaning that robs them of their force in the new environment. As we saw, the attraction of certain feelings and intuitions has a totally different significance in the two stances. This totality forces a choice; one cannot accord the two rival meanings to these crucial features at the same time. You can't really sit on the fence, because you need some reading of these features to get on with life. The attraction of theism can be lived as a temptation, or as a promise, but not easily as both at once (unless, of course, you change the meaning of "temptation" or "promise"). The option is forced in James's terms.

(2) And yet both these stances remain possible to many people in our world. Secularists once hoped that with the advance of science and enlightenment, and the articulation of a new, humanist ethic, the illusory nature of religion would be more and more apparent, and its attractions would fade, indeed, give way to repulsion. Many believers thought that unbelief was so clearly a willed blindness that people would one day wake up and see through it once and for all. But this is not how it has worked out, not even perhaps how it could work out. People go on feeling a sense of unease at the world of unbelief: some sense that something big, something important has been left out, some level of profound desire has been ignored, some greater reality outside us has been closed off. The articulations given to this unease are very varied, but it persists, and they recur in ever more ramified forms. But at the same time, the sense of dignity, control, adulthood, autonomy, connected to unbelief go on attract-

ing people, and seem set to do so into an indefinite future.

What is more, a close attention to the debate seems to indicate that most people feel both pulls. They have to go one way, but they never fully shake off the call of the other. So the faith of believers is fragilized, not just by the fact that other people, equally intelligent, often equally good and dedicated, disagree with them, but also by the fact that they can still see themselves as reflected in the other perspective, that is, as drawn by a too-indulgent view of things. For what believer doesn't have the sense that her view of God is too simple, too anthropocentric, too indulgent? We all lie to some extent "cowering" under "the agnostic vetoes upon faith as something weak and shameful" (204).

On the other side, the call to faith is still there as an understood temptation. Even if we think that it no longer applies to us, we see it as drawing others. Otherwise the ethics of belief would be incomprehensible.

Part of the great continuing interest of James's century-old work is that it lays out the dynamics of this battle so well and clearly. He is on one side, but he helps you imagine what it's like to be on either. In one way, we might interpret him as having wanted to show that you ought to come down on one side, the stronger thesis I offered above; but the weaker reading is just that he wanted to rebut the idea that reason forces you to the agnostic choice. As Edward Madden puts it in the Introduction to *The Will to Believe*, James might be seen as arguing really for a "right to believe" (WB xiii–xxiv); the right to follow one's own gut instinct in this domain, free of an intimidation grounded in invalid arguments.

What is especially striking about this account is that it brings out the bare issue so starkly, uncomplicated by further questions. It gives a stripped-down version of the debate; and this in two ways, both of which connect centrally to James's take on religion as experience.

First, precisely because he abandons so much of the traditional ground of religion, because he has no use for collective connections through sacraments or ways of life, because the intellectual articulations are made secondary, the key point—what to make of the gut instinct that there is something more?—stands out very clearly.

And this allows us to see the second way in which

James focuses the debate. It is after all to do with religious experience, albeit in a sense somewhat more generic than James's. As one stands on the cusp between the two great options, it is all a matter of the sense you have that there is something more, bigger, outside you. Now whether, granted you take the faith branch, this remains "religious experience" in James's special sense, steering clear of collective connections and overtheorization, is a question yet to be determined. But as you stand on the cusp, all you have to go on is a (very likely poorly articulated) gut feeling.

James is our great philosopher of the cusp. He tells us more than anyone else about what it's like to stand in that open space and feel the winds pulling you now here, now there. He describes a crucial site of modernity and articulates the decisive drama enacted there. It took very exceptional qualities to do this. Very likely it needed someone who had been through a searing experience of "morbidity" and had come out the other side. But it also needed someone of wide sympathy, and extraordinary powers of phenomenological description; further, it needed someone who could feel and articulate the continuing ambivalence in himself.[7] It probably also needed someone who had ultimately come down, with whatever inner tremors, on the faith side; but this may be a bit of believers' chauvinism that I am adding to the equation.

In any event, it is because he stands so nakedly and so volubly in this exposed spot that his work has resonated for a hundred years, and will go on doing so for many years to come.

3

RELIGION
TODAY

3

Starting from this sense of James's uniqueness, we can return to the question, What does he have to tell us about religion today?

I have talked of James as describing the point of choice, the flip-over point where one can go from belief to unbelief or the reverse. But we also saw earlier that he has a very partial view of what religion is in our day. In a sense, there is a connection between these two points, because the very stripped-down picture of religious experience helps to focus the bare point of choice more starkly.

But perhaps one might think that James was prescient in putting things this way. Supposing we are living in a world in which more and more people are forced out of comfortable niches in which they can be believers or unbelievers with minimal challenge from their surroundings; supposing more and more people are pushed on to the cusp that James so well described; won't this world be one whose spiritual pattern more and more depends on personal decisions that move people one way or another at the point of choice? And won't this world resemble the rather stripped-down religious landscape of James? We can easily imagine this being true in two senses: that this world will be more secular and neutral in its public life, that is, that it will be less and less possible to allow the social cadre in which these individual decisions take place to reflect one or other position; and that the spiritual landscape created by all these individual decisions will be less and less hospitable to collective connections.

Now there is some truth to both of these surmises, but they don't add up to the global vindication of James's idea of religious experience that they might be thought to at first blush.

SECULARIZATION OF THE PUBLIC SPHERE

We used to live in societies in which the presence of God was unavoidable; authority itself was bound up with the divine, and various invocations of God were inseparable from public life. But there was more than one form of this in our past. Between the sixteenth and the nineteenth centuries, we moved from an original model, which was alive in the Middle Ages, and in a number of nonwestern cultures, to another, very different one.

The earlier one was connected to what one might call an "enchanted world," an antonym to Max Weber's term "disenchanted." In an enchanted world there is a strong contrast between sacred and profane. By the sacred, I mean certain places, like churches; certain times, like high feasts; certain actions, like saying the Mass, in which the divine or the holy is present. As against these, other places, times, actions count as profane.

In an enchanted world, there is an obvious way in which God can be present in society: in the loci of the sacred. And the political society can be closely connected to these, and can itself be thought to exist on a higher plane. Ernst Kantorowicz tells us that one of the first uses of the term "mystical body" in European history referred to the French kingdom.[1] The king himself could be one of the links between the planes, represented respectively by the king's mortal and undying bodies.

Or to talk a slightly different language, in these earlier societies the kingdom existed not only in ordinary, secular time, in which a strong transitivity rule held, but also in higher times. There are, of course, different kinds of higher times—Platonist eternity, where there is a level at which we are beyond the flux altogether;

God's eternity as understood in the Christian tradition, a kind of gathering of time together; and various times of origins, in Mircea Eliade's sense.

With advancing disenchantment, especially in Protestant societies, another model took shape, with relation both to the cosmos and to the polity. In this the notion of design was crucial. In regard to the cosmos, there was a shift from the enchanted world to a cosmos conceived in conformity with post-Newtonian science, in which there is absolutely no possibility of higher meanings being *expressed* in the universe around us. But there is still, with someone like Newton himself, for instance, a strong sense that the universe declares the glory of God. This is evident in its design, its beauty, its regularity, but also in its having evidently been shaped to conduce to the welfare of God's creatures, particularly of ourselves, the superior creatures who cap it all off. Now the presence of God no longer lies in the sacred, because this category fades in a disenchanted world. But he can be thought to be no less powerfully present through his design.

The presence of God in the cosmos is matched by the idea of his presence in the polity. Here an analogous change takes place. The divine isn't there in a King who straddles the planes. But it can be present to the extent that we build a society that plainly follows God's design. This mode of presence can be filled in with an idea of moral order that is seen as established by God, in the way invoked, for instance, in the American Declaration of Independence: men have been created equal, and have been endowed by their creator with certain inalienable rights.

The idea of moral order which is expressed in this Declaration, and which has since become dominant in our world, is quite different from the orders that preceded it, because it starts from individuals and doesn't see these as set a priori within a hierarchical order, outside of which they wouldn't be fully human agents. Its members are not agents who are essentially embedded in a society that in turn reflects and connects with the cosmos, but rather disembedded individuals who come to associate together. The design underlying the association is that each, in pursuing his or her own purposes in life, acts to benefit others mutually. It calls for a society structured for mutual benefit, in which each respects the rights of others and offers them mutual help of certain kinds. The most influential early articulator of this formula is John Locke, but the basic conception of such an order of mutual service has come down to us through a series of variants, including more radical ones, such as those presented by Rousseau and Marx.

But in the earlier days, when the plan was understood as providential, and the order seen as natural law, which is the same as the law of God, building a society that fulfills these requirements was seen as fulfilling the design of God. To live in such a society was to live in one where God was present, not at all in the way that belonged to the enchanted world, through the sacred, but because we were following his design. God is present as the designer of the way we live. We see ourselves, to quote a famous phrase, as "one people under God."

In thus taking the United States as a paradigm case of this new idea of order, I am following Robert Bellah's tremendously fertile idea of an American "civil religion." Of course, the concept is understandably and rightly contested today, because some of the conditions of this religion are now being challenged, but there is no doubt that Bellah has captured something essential about American society, both at its inception and for about two centuries thereafter.

The fundamental idea, that America had a vocation to carry out God's purposes, which alone makes sense of the passages Bellah quotes, for instance, from Kennedy's Inaugural Address, and even more from Lincoln's Second Inaugural, and which can seem strange and threatening to many unbelievers in America today, has to be understood in relation to this conception of an order of free, rights-bearing individuals. This was what was invoked in the Declaration of Independence, which appealed to "the Laws of Nature and of Nature's God." The rightness of these laws, for both deists and theists, was grounded in their being part of the providential design. What the activism of the American Revolutionaries added to this was a view of history as the theater in which this design was to be progressively realized, and of their own society as the place where this realization was to be consummated— what Lincoln would later refer to as "the last, best hope of earth." It was this notion of themselves as fulfilling divine purposes that, along with the biblical culture of Protestant America, facilitated the analogy with ancient Israel that often recurs in American official rhetoric of the early days.[2]

The confusion today arises from the fact that there is both continuity and discontinuity. What continues is the importance of some form of the modern idea of moral order. It is this which gives the sense that Americans are still operating on the same principles as the

Founders. The rift comes from the fact that what makes this order the right one is, for many though not by any means for all, no longer God's providence; the order is grounded in nature alone, or in some concept of civilization, or even in supposedly unchallengeable a priori principles, often inspired by Kant. So that some Americans want to rescue the Constitution from God, whereas others, with deeper historical roots, see this desire as doing violence to it. Hence the contemporary American Kulturkampf.

But the U.S. path to modernity, though considered paradigmatic by many Americans, is in fact rather exceptional. A secularization of the public sphere has come about in rather different ways elsewhere.

Thus in Catholic societies, the old model of presence lasted much longer. True, it was affected by disenchantment, and became more and more a compromise, in which the hierarchical order was in some sense treated as untouchable and the king as sacred, but in which also elements of functional justification began to creep in, where monarchical rule was argued to be indispensable for order, for example. We can think of this as the "baroque" compromise.

The path to what we are now living today passes out of both of these forms of divine presence in society into something different. The path out of the Catholic "baroque" went through a catastrophic revolutionary overturn. But the "Protestant" one was smoother, and therefore harder in some ways to trace. It is, of course, this one which will cast most light on James's situation.

David Martin, in a number of insightful works, has developed an interesting account of the "Protestant," more particularly "anglophone" path.[3] This path comes about in societies in which the reigning forms of social imaginary center more and more on the order of mutual benefit, and the "baroque" order is seen as distant and somewhat abhorrent, in short "papist."

In keeping with this outlook, it seems more and more evident in these cultures that valid religious adherence can only be voluntary. Forcing it has less and less legitimacy. And so popular alienation from élite-dominated religion can take the form of new voluntary associations, rather different from the earlier churches. The prototype of these is the Wesleyan Methodists, but the real explosion in such free churches occurs in the United States at the end of the eighteenth century and transforms the face of American religion.

With the Methodists, we have something new, neither a church nor a sect, but a protoform of what we now call a "denomination." A "church" in this Troeltschian sense claims to gather within it all members of society; as with the Catholic church, it sees its vocation as being the church for everyone. Some of the main Reformation churches had the same aspiration, and often managed to take with them into dissidence whole societies, for instance, in Germany, Scandinavia, and initially England as well.

But even what we call "sects" after Troeltsch, which concentrated on the "saved," those who really deserved to be members, were in a sense frustrated churches. That is, either like Presbyterians in England, they aspired to take over the one national church; or like some Anabaptists, they despaired of the larger society, but just for that reason tried to reduce their contacts with it to a minimum. They still tried to circumscribe a zone in which they defined religious life.

At its beginning, the Methodist movement didn't aspire to churchhood, just to being a current within the national Church of England. They would practice their own kind of spirituality, but within a broader body that included others. Their desired status was analogous in some ways to that of religious orders in the Catholic church. Something of this sense of legitimate difference carries over when they are forced out, and becomes the standard outlook that distinguishes the denomination, dominant on the U.S. scene.

Denominations are like affinity groups. They don't see their differences from (at least some) others as make-or-break, salvation-or-damnation issues. Their way is better for them, may even be seen as better tout court, but doesn't cut them off from other recognized denominations. They thus exist in a space of other "churches," such that in another, more general sense, the whole group of these make up "the church." The injunction to worship in the church of your choice is an injunction to belong to the "church" in this broader sense, the limits of permitted choice defining its boundaries.

In earlier days on the American scene, Catholics were outside these limits, as they are still for many today. But for others, the limits have widened to include Jews as part of a common adhesion to Judeo-Christian theism.

So it is a feature of denominationalism that, just because one's own church does not include all the faithful, there is a sense of belonging to a wider, less structured whole which does. And this can find at least partial expression in the state. That is, the members of mutually recognizing denominations can form a people "under God," with the sense of acting according to the demands of God in forming and maintaining their state, as in the case of the American "civil religion" alluded to above. Indeed, insofar as the divine design includes freedom, this can be interpreted as calling for an openness to a plurality of denominations.

This sense of a providential political mission has been very strong among American Protestants, and remains alive today. But something analogous also developed in Britain. Linda Colley has claimed that a kind of British nationalism developed in the eighteenth century, part of which formed around the sense of a shared Protestantism, which overarched differences in actual confession.[4] This built on a previous self-identification of the English with the Protestant cause, in a world where the major threats to national security came from large "papist" powers.

So in one way, a denominational identity tends to separate religion from the state. A denomination cannot be a national church, and its members can't accept and join whatever claims to be the national church. Denominationalism implies that churches are all equally options, and thrives best in a régime of separation of church and state, de facto if not de jure. But on another level, the political entity can be identified with the broader, overarching "church," and this can be a crucial element in its patriotism.

This of course gives us a situation very different from the "Durkheimian" one prevailing in some Catholic countries, where the social sacred is defined and served by the church. For one thing, in this disenchanted Protestant setting, there is no more "sacred" in the earlier sense, in which certain places, times, people, acts are distinguished as such from the profane. For another, no one church can uniquely define and celebrate the link of the political society and divine providence.

Of course, I am speaking here of an ideal type, one which in this regard is fully realized in the United States. The British situation is muddied by the continued existence of national churches, which in one case (the Anglican Church) goes on assuming a ceremonial role, which in type and even in many of its ritual details is a legacy of its Catholic, medieval past. But mass enjoyment of this ceremonial has long been unhooked from identification with this church.

I will call this kind of link between religion and the state "neo-Durkheimian," contrasting on the one hand with the "paleo-Durkheimian" mode of "baroque"

Catholic societies, and on the other with more recent forms in which the spiritual dimension of existence is quite unhooked from the political. The "paleo" phase corresponds to a situation in which a sense of the ontic dependence of the state on God and higher times is still alive, even though it may be weakened by disenchantment and an instrumental spirit; whereas in "neo" societies, God is present because it is his design around which society is organized. It is this which we concur on as the identifying common description of our society, what we could call its "political identity."

If we look at this "anglophone" trajectory, we can see that, unlike the "baroque" one, where the church almost inevitably generated counterforces, it can sustain a high level of religious belief and practice. Resentment at the power of élites, and estrangement from their spiritual style, can find expression in another mode of Christian life and worship. Popular groups can find and live by their own spiritual style, as the "enthusiastic" Methodists did in eighteenth-century England, and the Baptists did in the rural United States, and evangelicals and Pentecostals are doing today in Latin America, Africa, and Asia. Alienation from a Northeast dominated by genteel Episcopalians and Presbyterians can take the form of passionate born-again evangelicalism in the South and West.

At the same time, belief is sustained by the "neo-Durkheimian" identification with the state. Over a long period, for many of the English, Christianity of a certain Protestant variety was identified with certain moral standards, often summed in the word "decency,"[5] and England was thought to be the preeminent carrier of this variety on the world scene. This was what we could call the "established synthesis." English patriotism was built for many around this complex of beliefs and norms. Many Protestant Americans, and latterly some Catholic ones, have thought that the United States has a providential mission to spread liberal democracy among the rest of humankind.

The point here can perhaps be generalized. In the course of modern history, confessional allegiances have come to be woven into the sense of identity of certain ethnic, national, class, or regional groups. Britain and the United States are powerful, independent nations. But this kind of identification often happens with marginal or oppressed populations. The Polish and Irish Catholic identities are well-known cases in point. The erstwhile French-Canadian one is another.

The link here between group and confession is not the paleo-Durkheimian one of the "baroque" hierarchy, even though it is the same Catholic church which is involved. Throne and altar can't be allied, because the throne is alien, not just when it is Lutheran, Anglican, or Orthodox, but even when it is Catholic (Vienna). Resentment at élites becomes marginal to the extent that these élites lose power and privilege. But the sense of national domination and oppression, the sense of virtue in suffering and struggle, is deeply interwoven with the religious belief and allegiance— even to the point of such rhetorical excesses as the depiction of Poland as "Christ crucified among the nations." The result is what I'm calling a "neo-Durkheimian" effect, where the senses of belonging to group and confession are fused, and the moral issues of the group's history tend to be coded in religious categories. (The rival language for oppressed people was always that of the French Revolution. This had its moments in each of the subaltern nations mentioned here: the United Irish, Papineau's rebellion in 1837, Dabrowski's legion; but in each case the Catholic coding later took the upper hand.)

Where this effect takes hold, a potential decline in belief and practice is retarded or fails to occur. This easily gives rise to a misunderstanding in the climate of contemporary sociology with its rather "secular" mindset. One is tempted to say of these situations, as well as the anglophone nations above, that religion is performing an "integrating function." The slide is easy to the thesis that religious belief is the dependent variable here, its integrative function being the explanatory factor.

But I think it would be less distortive to say that the religious language is the one in which people find it meaningful to code their strong moral and political experience, either of oppression or of successful state-building around certain moral principles. The point of citing the different predicaments of Polish or Irish peasants or workers, on one hand, and their Spanish or French counterparts on the other, is that the first offered inducements and little resistance to coding in a Catholic language, whereas life in a "baroque" régime generates experiences that are strong deterrents to doing so.

THE NEW INDIVIDUALISM

Something has happened in the last half-century, perhaps even less, which has profoundly altered the conditions of belief in our societies. We are now at a rather new phase of religious life, and one that James in a sense prefigured.

I believe, along with many others, that our North Atlantic civilization has been undergoing a cultural revolution in recent decades. The 1960s provide perhaps the hinge moment, at least symbolically. It is on one hand an individuating revolution, which may sound strange, because our modern age was already based on a certain individualism. But this has shifted on to a new axis, without deserting the others. As well as moral/spiritual, and instrumental individualisms, we now have a widespread "expressive" individualism. This is, of course, not totally new. Expressivism was the invention of the Romantic period in the late eighteenth century. Intellectual and artistic élites searched for the authentic way of living or expressing themselves throughout the nineteenth century. What is new is that this kind of self-orientation seems to have become a mass phenomenon.

Its most obvious external manifestation has perhaps been the consumer revolution. With postwar affluence, and the diffusion of what many had considered luxuries before, came a new concentration on private space, and the means to fill it, which began distending the relations of previously close-knit working-class or peasant communities, even of extended families.[6] Modes of mutual help dropped off, perhaps partly because of the receding of dire necessity. People concentrated more on their own lives and those of their nuclear families. They moved to new towns or suburbs, lived more on their own, tried to make a life out of the ever-growing gamut of new goods and services on offer, from washing machines to packaged holidays, and the freer individual lifestyles they facilitated. The "pursuit of happiness" took on new, more immediate meaning, with a growing range of easily available means. And in this newly individuated space, the customer was encouraged more and more to express her taste, furnishing her space according to her own needs and affinities, as only the rich had been able to do in previous eras.

One important facet of this new consumer culture was the creation of a special youth market, with a flood of new goods, from clothes to records, aimed at an age bracket that ranged over adolescents and young adults. The advertising deployed to sell these goods in symbiosis with the youth culture helped create a new kind of consciousness of youth as a stage in life, between childhood and an adulthood tied down by responsibility. This was not, of course, without precedent. Many earlier societies had marked out such a stage in the life cycle, with its own special groupings and rituals; and upper-class youth had enjoyed their student days and (sometimes) fraternities. Indeed, with the expansion of urban life and the consolidation of national cultures, upper- and middle-class youth began to become conscious of itself as a social reality toward the end of the nineteenth century. Youth even becomes a political reference point or a basis of mobilization, as one sees with the German Jugendbewegung, and later with Fascist invocation of "Giovinezza" in their famous marching song. But this self-demarcation of youth was a break with the working-class culture of the nineteenth and early twentieth centuries, where the necessities of life seemed to exclude such a time-out after childhood and before the serious business of earning began.

The current youth culture is defined, both by the way advertising is pitched at it, and to a great degree autonomously, as expressivist. The styles of dress adopted, the kinds of music listened to, give expression to the personality, to the affinities of the chooser, within a wide space of fashion in which one's choice could align one with thousands, even millions of others.

If we move from these external facts about postwar consumerism to the self-understandings that went along with them, we see a steady spread of what I have called the culture of "authenticity."[7] I mean the understanding of life that emerged with the Romantic expressivism of the late eighteenth century, that each of us has his or her own way of realizing one's own humanity, and that it is important to find and live out one's own, as against surrendering to conformity with a model imposed from outside, by society, or the previous generation, or religious or political authority.

This had been the standpoint of many intellectuals and artists during the nineteenth and early twentieth centuries. One can trace the strengthening, even radicalization of this ethos among some cultural élites throughout this period, a growing sense of the right, even duty, to resist "bourgeois" or established codes and standards, to declare openly for the art and the mode of life that they felt inspired to create and live. The defining of its own ethos by the Bloomsbury milieu was an important stage on this road in early twentieth-century England, and the sense of the epochal change is reflected in the famous words of Virginia Woolf: "On or about December 1910, human nature changed."[8] A somewhat parallel moment comes with André Gide's "coming out" as a homosexual in the 1920s, a move in which desire, morality, and a sense of integrity came together. It is not just that Gide no longer felt the need to maintain a false front; it is that after a long struggle he was this front as a wrong that he was inflicting on himself, and on others who labored under similar disguises.[9]

But it was only in the era after the Second World War that this ethic of authenticity began to shape the outlook of society in general. Expressions like "do your own thing" became current; a beer commercial of the early 1970s enjoined us to "be yourselves in the world of today." A simplified expressivism infiltrated everywhere. Therapies proliferated that promised to help you find yourself, realize yourself, release your true self, and so on.

The new expressivist self-awareness brings to the fore a different kind of social imaginary. I have spoken elsewhere about the typically modern, "horizontal" forms of social imaginary, in which people grasp themselves and great numbers of others as existing and acting simultaneously.[10] The three widely recognized such forms are the economy, the public sphere, and the sovereign people. But the space of fashion mentioned above is an example of a fourth structure of simultaneity. It is unlike the public sphere and the sovereign people, because these are sites of common action. In this respect, it is like the economy, where a host of individual actions concatenate. But it is different from this as well, because our actions relate in the space of fashion in a particular way. I wear my own kind of hat, but in doing so I am displaying my style to all of you, and in this I am responding to your self-display, even as you will respond to mine. The space of fashion is one in which we sustain a language together of signs and meanings, which is constantly changing, but which at any moment is the background needed to give our gestures the sense they have. If my hat can express my particular kind of cocky yet understated self-display, this is because of how the common language of style has evolved between us up to this point. My gesture can change it, and then your responding stylistic move will take its meaning from the new contour the language takes on.

The resulting general structure is not that of a common action, but rather of mutual display. It matters to each of us as we act that the others are there, as witnesses of what we are doing, and thus as co-determiners of the meaning of our action.

Spaces of this kind become more and more important in modern urban society, where large numbers of people rub shoulders, unknown to each other, without dealings with each other, and yet affecting each other, forming the inescapable context of each other's lives. As against the everyday rush to work on the subway, where the others can sink to the status of obstacles in my way, city life has developed other ways of being-with, for instance, as we each take our Sunday walk in the park; or as we mingle at the summer street-festival, or in the stadium before the playoff game. Here each individual or small group acts on its own, but aware that its display says something to the others, will be responded to by them, will help build a common mood or tone that will color everyone's actions.

Here a host of urban monads hover on the boundary between solipsism and communication. My loud remarks and gestures are overtly addressed only to my immediate companions, my family group is sedately walking, engaged in our own Sunday outing, but all the time we are aware of this common space that we are building, in which the messages that cross take their meaning. This strange zone between loneliness and communication strongly impressed many of the early observers of this phenomenon as it arose in the nineteenth century. We can think of some of the paintings of Manet, or of Baudelaire's fascination with the urban scene, in the roles of flâneur and dandy, uniting observation and display.

Of course, these nineteenth-century urban spaces were topical; that is, all the participants were in the same place, in sight of each other. But twentieth-century communications have produced metatopical variants, when, for instance, we watch the Olympics or Princess Di's funeral on television, aware that millions of others are with us in this activity. The meaning of our participation in the event is shaped by the whole vast dispersed audience we share it with.

Just because these spaces hover between solitude and togetherness, they may sometimes flip over into common action; and indeed, the moment when they do so may be hard to pinpoint. As we rise as one to cheer the crucial third-period goal, we have undoubtedly become a common agent; and we may try to prolong this when we leave the stadium by marching and chanting, or even wreaking various forms of mayhem together. The cheering crowd at a rock festival is similarly fused. There is a heightened excitement at these moments of fusion, reminiscent of Carnival or of some of the other great collective rituals of earlier days. So that some have seen these moments as among the new forms of religion in our world.[11] And Durkheim gave an important place to these times of collective effervescence as founding moments of society and the sacred.[12] In any case, these moments seem to respond to some important felt need of today's "lonely crowd."

And so the new, more individualized pursuit of happiness, loosening some of the ties and common lifeways of the past, the spread of expressive individualism and the culture of authenticity, the increased importance of these spaces of mutual display, all these seem to point to a new way of being together in society. This expressive individualism, which has been growing since the war, is obviously stronger in some milieus than in others, stronger among youth than among older people, stronger among those who were formed in the 1960s and 1970s; but overall it seems steadily to advance.

How is it altering our social imaginary? Here I can only sketch an ideal type, because we're dealing with a gradual process, in which the new coexists with the old.

Our self-understandings as sovereign peoples hasn't been displaced by this new individualism. And as for the modern moral order of mutual benefit, this has been if anything strengthened. Or perhaps, better put, it has taken on a somewhat different form. Certainly it is clear that the ideals of fairness, of mutual respect of each other's freedom, are as strong among young people today as they ever were. Indeed, precisely the soft relativism that seems to accompany the ethic of authenticity: let each person do his or her own thing, and we shouldn't criticize each other's "values"; this is predicated on a firm ethical base, indeed, demanded by it. One shouldn't criticize others' values, because they have a right to live their own life as you do. The sin that is not tolerated is intolerance. This injunction emerges clearly from the ethic of freedom and mutual benefit.[13]

Where the new twist comes in, evident in the "relativism," is that this injunction stands alone, whereas it used to be surrounded and contained by others. For Locke, the law of nature needed to be inculcated in people by strong discipline; so although the goal was individual freedom, there was no felt incompatibility between this and the need for strong, commonly enforced virtues of character. On the contrary, it seemed evident that without these, the régime of mutual respect couldn't survive. It took a long time before John Stuart Mill could enunciate what has come to be called the "harm principle," that no one has a right to interfere with me for my own good, but only to prevent harm to others. In his day, this was far from generally accepted; it seemed the path to libertinism.

But today the harm principle is widely accepted, and seems the formula demanded by the dominant expressive individualism. (It is perhaps not an accident that Mill's arguments also drew on expressivist sources, in the person of Humboldt.)

Indeed, the "pursuit of (individual) happiness" took on a new meaning in the postwar period. Of course, it has been integral to liberalism since the American Revolution, which enshrined it as one of a trinity of basic rights. But in the first century of the American republic, it was inscribed within certain taken-for-granted boundaries. First there was the citizen ethic, centered on the good of self-rule, which Americans were meant to live up to. But beyond this were certain basic demands of sexual morality, of what later would be called "family values," as well as the values of hard work and productivity, which gave a framework to the pursuit of individual good. To move outside of these was not so much to seek one's happiness, as to head toward perdition. There seemed therefore nothing contrary to the three basic rights enshrined by the Declaration of Independence in society's striving to inculcate, even in certain cases (such as sexual morality) to enforce these norms. European societies were perhaps less keen than the Americans to enforce various modes of social conformity, but their code was if anything even more restrictive.

The erosion of these limits on individual fulfillment has been in some cases gradual, with oscillations but with an unmistakable general tendency over the long run. Michael Sandel has noted that the concern for the citizen ethic was much more prominent in the first century of U.S. history. Brandeis could argue the antitrust case at the beginning of the twentieth century partly on the ground that large combines were "eroding the moral and civic capacities that equip workers to think like citizens."[14] But as the twenty-first century begins, such considerations increasingly take a back seat. Courts have become more concerned to defend the "privacy" of the individual.

But it is really in the period after the Second World War that the limits on the pursuit of individual happiness were most clearly set aside, particularly in sexual matters but in other domains as well. The U.S. Supreme Court decisions invoking privacy, and thereby restricting the range of the criminal law, provide a clear example. Something similar happened with the revisions of the Canadian Criminal Code under Pierre Trudeau, which expressed his principle that "the State has no business in the bedrooms of the nation." Michel Winock notes the change in "mentalités" in France during the 1970s. "La levée des censures, la 'libéralisation des moeurs' . . . entra dans la loi," with the legalization of abortion, divorce reform, authorization of pornographic films, and so on.[15] This evolution has occurred in virtually all Atlantic societies.

In fact the need to train character has receded even farther into the background, as though the morality of mutual respect were embedded in the ideal of authentic self-fulfillment itself; which is how undoubtedly many young people experience it today, oblivious of how the terrible twentieth-century aberrations of Fascism and extreme nationalism have also drunk at the expressivist source.

All this perhaps reflects the degree to which these

principles of mutual respect for rights have become embedded in our cultures in the Atlantic world, forming the background against which many of our political and legal procedures of rights-retrieval and nondiscrimination seem totally legitimate, even though we vigorously dispute their detailed application. But it also reflects the way in which rights-consciousness has become more loosely linked to the sense of belonging to a particular political community, which has both positive and negative sides.

I leave aside the pros and cons here to concentrate on what is relevant to our purposes, which we could describe as the imagined place of the sacred, in the widest sense. Drawing an ideal type of this new social imaginary of expressive individualism, we could say that it was quite non-Durkheimian.

Under the paleo-Durkheimian dispensation, my connection to the sacred entailed my belonging to a church, in principle coextensive with society, although in fact there were perhaps tolerated outsiders, and as yet undisciplined heretics. The neo-Durkheimian dispensation saw me enter the denomination of my choice, but that in turn connected me to a broader, more elusive "church," and, more important, to a political entity with a providential role to play. In both these cases, there was a link between adhering to God and belonging to the state—hence my epithet "Durkheimian."

The neo-Durkheimian mode involves an important step toward the individual and the right of choice. One joins a denomination because it seems right to one. And indeed, it now comes to seem that there is no way of being in the "church" except through such a choice. Whereas under paleo-Durkheimian rules one can—and did—demand that people be forcibly integrated, be rightly connected with God against their will, this now makes no sense. Coercion comes to seem not only wrong, but absurd and thus obscene. We saw an important watershed in the development of this consciousness in the reaction of educated Europe to the revocation of the Edict of Nantes. Even the pope thought it was a mistake.

But the expressivist outlook takes this a stage further. The religious life or practice that I become part of not only must be my choice, but must speak to me; it must make sense in terms of my spiritual development as I understand this. This takes us further. The choice of denomination was understood to take place within a fixed cadre, say that of the Apostles' Creed, the faith of the broader "church." Within this framework of belief, I choose the church in which I feel most comfortable. But if the focus is going now to be on my spiritual path, thus on what insights come to me in the subtler languages that I find meaningful, then maintaining this or any other framework becomes increasingly difficult.

But this means that my place in the broader "church" may not be that relevant for me, and along with this, my placing in the "people under God," or other such political agency with a providential role. In the new expressivist dispensation, there is no necessary embedding of our link to the sacred in any particular broader framework, whether "church" or state.

This is why the developments of recent decades in France have been so destabilizing for both sides of the old "guerre franco-française." Not only did the church see a sharp drop in adherence, but young people began to drop out of the rival Jacobin and/or Communist worldviews as well. In keeping with the dynamic of baroque, paleo-Durkheimian clericalism, the struggle threw up a kind of humanism that aspired in its own way to be a kind of national "church," that of the Republic and its principles, the framework within which people would hold their different metaphysical and (if they insisted) religious views. The Republic played a kind of neo-Durkheimian dispensation against the paleo-Durkheimianism of the clerical monarchists. This tradition even took over the term "sacred" for itself. (Think of "l'union sacrée," of "la main sacrilège" that killed Marat, and so on. This usage obviously facilitated Durkheim's theoretical use of the term to overarch both *ancien régime* and republic.) It is not surprising that both Catholicism and this brand of republicanism undergo defections in the new post-Durkheimian dispensation of expressive individualism.

This new dispensation changes utterly the ways in which ideals of order used to be interwoven with the polemic between belief and unbelief. What has changed to make this much less the case is not only that we have achieved a broad consensus on our ideal of moral order. It is also that in our post-Durkheimian dispensation, the "sacred," either religious or "laïque," has become uncoupled from our political allegiance. It was the rivalry between two such kinds of global allegiance that animated the "guerre franco-française." It was also this older dispensation which could send masses of men into the trenches to fight for their country in 1914, and keep them there, with few desertions and rare instances of mutiny, for over four years.[16]

I speak of this in the past tense, because in many of these same countries which were the prime belligerents in this war the new dispensation has probably made this kind of thing impossible. But it is also clear that the geographic area for which this holds true is limited. Down in the Balkans, not that much has changed since the wars that broke out in 1911. And we should not be too sanguine in believing that the change is irreversible even in the core North Atlantic societies.

Paleo-, neo-, post-Durkheimian describe ideal types. My claim is not that any of these provides the total description, but that our history has moved through these dispensations, and that the latter has come more and more to color our age.

That the new dispensation doesn't provide the whole story is readily evident from the struggles in contemporary society. In a sense, part of what drove the Moral Majority and motivates the Christian right in the United States is an aspiration to reestablish something of the fractured neo-Durkheimian understanding that used to define the nation, where being

American would once more have a connection with theism, with being "one people under God," or at least with the ethic which was interwoven with this. Similarly, much of the leadership of the Catholic church, led by the Vatican, is trying to resist the challenge to monolithic authority that is implicit in the new expressivist understanding of spirituality. And the Catholic church in the United States frequently lines up with the Christian right in attempts to reestablish earlier versions of the moral consensus that enjoyed in their day neo-Durkheimian religious grounding.[17]

But the very embattled nature of these attempts shows how we have slid out of the old dispensation. This shift goes a long way to explain the conditions of belief in our day.

Before examining this, however, I want to bring out how much the shift consorts with the logic of modern subjectification, and with what we might call the "buffered self." We already saw in the eighteenth century, at one of the important "branching points" mentioned in earlier, that one reaction to the cool, measured religion of the buffered identity was to stress feeling, emotion, a living faith that moves us. We see this with Pietism and Methodism. This is more important than theological correctness.

Of course, these movements wished to remain within orthodoxy, but it wouldn't be long before the emphasis shifted more and more toward the strength and the genuineness of the feelings rather than toward the nature of their object. Later in the century, the readers of *Émile* would admire above all the deep authentic sentiments of the characters.

There is a certain logic in this. Where before there was lots of passionate belief, and the life-and-death issues were doctrinal, now there came to be a widespread feeling that the very point of religion was being lost in the cool distance of even impeccable intellectual orthodoxy. One could connect with God only through passion. For those who felt this, the intensity of the passion became a major virtue, well worth some lack of accuracy in theological formulation. In an age dominated by disengaged reason, this virtue came to seem more and more crucial.

By the time of the Romantic period, the same issue had been somewhat transposed. Now it appeared to many that desiccated reason could not reach the ultimate truths in any form. What was needed was a subtler language that could make manifest the higher or the divine. But this language required for its force that it resonate with the writer or reader. Getting assent to some external formula was not the main thing; being able to generate the moving insight into higher reality was what was important. Deeply felt personal insight now became our most precious spiritual resource. For Schleiermacher, the crucial thing to explore was the powerful feeling of dependence on something greater. To give this reign and voice in oneself was more crucial than getting the right formula.

I believe that the present expressive outlook comes from that shift having penetrated in some general form deep into our culture. In an age that seems dominated by the "learned despisers of religion," in Schleiermacher's phrase, what is really valuable is spiritual insight/feeling. This will inevitably draw on a language that resonates very much with the person who possesses it. Thus the injunction would seem to be: let everyone follow his or her own path of spiritual inspiration. Don't be led off yours by the allegation that it doesn't fit with some orthodoxy.

Hence while in the original paleo-Durkheimian dispensation, people could easily feel that they had to obey the command to abandon their own religious instincts, because these, being at variance with orthodoxy, must be heretical or at least inferior; while those inhabiting a neo-Durkheimian world felt that their choice had to conform to the overall framework of the "church" or favored nation, so that even Unitarians and ethical societies presented themselves as denominations with services and sermons on Sunday; in the post-Durkheimian age many people are uncomprehending in face of the demand to conform. Just as in the neo-Durkheimian world, joining a church you don't believe in seems not just wrong but absurd, contradictory, so in the post-Durkheimian age seems the idea of adhering to a spirituality that doesn't present itself as your path, the one that moves and inspires you. For many people today, to set aside their own path in order to conform to some external authority just doesn't seem comprehensible as a form of spiritual life.[18] The injunction is, in the words of a speaker at a New Age festival: "Only accept what rings true to your own inner Self."[19]

Of course, this understanding of the place and nature of spirituality has pluralism built into it, not just pluralism within a certain doctrinal framework, but unlimited. Or rather, the limits are of another order; they are in a sense political, and flow from the moral order of freedom and mutual benefit. My spiritual path has to respect those of others; it must abide by the harm principle. With this restriction, one's path can range through those which require some community to live out, even national communities or would-be state churches, but it can also range beyond to those which require only the loosest of affinity groups, or just some servicing agency, like a source of advice and literature.

The a priori principle, that a valid answer to the religious quest must meet either the paleo- or neo-Durkheimian conditions (a church, or a "church" and/or society), has been abandoned in the new dispensation. The spiritual as such is no longer intrinsically related to society.

So much for the logic of the expressivist response to the buffered identity. But of course, this didn't have to work itself out as it has done. In certain societies at least, the principal catalyst for its having done so in recent decades seems to have been the new individual consumer culture released by postwar affluence. This seems to have had a tremendous appeal for populations that had been living since time out of mind under the grip of what appeared unchanging necessity, where the most optimistic horizon was maintaining a level of modest sufficiency and avoiding disaster. Yves Lambert has shown how this new culture at once loosened the tight community life of a Breton parish, and turned people from their dense communal-ritual life to the vigorous pursuit of personal prosperity. As one of his informants put it, "On n'a plus le temps de se soucier de ça [la religion], il y a trop de travail. Il faut de l'argent, du confort, tout ça, tout le monde est lancé là-dedans, et le reste, pffft!"[20]

These are connected movements. The new prosperity came along with better communications, and this opened horizons; but then the new pursuit of happiness drew people so strongly that they began to desert the older ritual life that was built around the community and its common efforts to survive in the physical and spiritual world. This ritual life then itself began to shrink, in part disappear, and there was less and less to hold those who might want to stay within it.[21]

It is almost as though the "conversion" was a response to a stronger form of magic, as earlier conversions had been. It is not that the religion of the villagers in Limerzel was exclusively concerned with economic survival and the defense against disaster, but that their faith had so woven together the concern for salvation with that for well-being, that the prospect of a new individual road to prosperity, proven and impressive, dislocated their whole previous outlook. Said another informant: "Pourquoi j'irais à la messe, qu'ils se disent, le voisin qui est à côté de moi, il réussit aussi bien que moi, peut-être même mieux, et il n'y va pas."[22]

In other words, the old outlook bound together a composite of concerns, worldly and otherworldly, which now fell apart quite decisively. It couldn't be reconstituted, and the faith has survived only among those who hold to it by evolving, as Lambert describes.[23] Something analogous happened in Québec, though this was a much more urbanized society, in the 1960s. Here the effect was delayed by the neo-Durkheimian link between national identity and Catholicism, but when this knot was untied, the falling off happened with a bewildering rapidity. The development has perhaps some affinities with what is taking place in contemporary Ireland, or what is beginning to emerge in Poland.

The corresponding slide in other Protestant, especially anglophone societies has been more gradual and less dramatic, perhaps because the new consumer culture developed more slowly and over a longer period. But in both Britain and America, the expressivist revolution of the 1960s seems to have accelerated things.

How to understand the impact of this whole shift on the place of religion in public space? It can perhaps be envisaged in this way. The invention of exclusive humanism in the eighteenth century created a new situation of pluralism, a culture fractured between religion and areligion (phase 1). The reactions not only to this humanism, but to the matrix (buffered identity, moral order) out of which it grew, multiplied the options in all directions (phase 2). But this pluralism operated and generated its new options for a long time largely within certain élite groups, intellectuals and artists.

Early on, especially in Catholic countries, there arose political movements of militant humanism that tried to carry unbelief to the masses, with rather modest success; and religious alienation also detached some strata of the common people from the church without necessarily offering them an alternative. On the other side, large numbers of people were either held outside this pluralist, fractured culture; or, if on the fringes of it, were held strongly within the believing option, by different modes of Durkheimian dispensation, whereby a given religious option was closely linked to their insertion in their society. This could be of the paleo type, which although it began to decay rapidly on the level of the whole society could still be very operative in rural areas at the level of the local community, as in Lambert's Limerzel. Or it could be of the neo type, as in the triumphant sense of national providence, or among oppressed groups, defending a threatened identity against power of another religious stripe (including atheism in the case of recent Poland), or among immigrant groups.

My hypothesis is that the postwar slide in our social imaginary more and more into a post-Durkheimian age has destabilized and undermined the various Durkheimian dispensations. This has had the effect of either gradually releasing people to be recruited into the fractured culture or, in the case where the new consumer culture has quite dislocated the earlier outlook, of explosively expelling people into this fractured world.

The measurable, external results are as we might expect: first, a rise in the number of those who state themselves to be atheists, agnostics, or to have no religion, in many countries, including Britain, France, the United States, and Australia.[24] But beyond this, the gamut of intermediate positions greatly widens: many people drop out of active practice while still declaring themselves as belonging to some confession or believing in God. On another dimension, the gamut of beliefs in something beyond widens, with fewer declaring belief in a personal God while more hold to something like an impersonal force;[25] in other words, a wider range of people express religious beliefs that move outside Christian orthodoxy. Following in this line is the growth of non-Christian religions, particularly those originating in the Orient, and the proliferation of New Age modes of practice, of views that bridge the humanist/spiritual boundary, of practices that link spirituality and therapy. On top of this, more and more people adopt what would earlier have been seen as untenable positions; for example, they consider themselves Catholic while not accepting many crucial dogmas, or they combine Christianity with Buddhism, or they pray while not being certain they believe. This is not to say that people didn't occupy positions like this in the past; just that now it seems to be easier to be upfront about it. In reaction to all this, Christian faith is in the process of redefining and recomposing itself in various ways, from Vatican II to the charismatic movements. All this represents the consequence of expressivist culture as it affects our world. It has created a quite new predicament.[26]

4

SO WAS
JAMES RIGHT?

4

It might seem that our post-Durkheimian world is a paradigmatically Jamesian one. Individuals make what they can of their "religious experience," without too much concern for how it all fits together at the level of society or how it affects the fate of different churches.

In one way, James is very close to the spirit of contemporary society. He was already living in his own post-Durkheimian dispensation. But in another way, he is still missing something important. I want to mention three key phenomena today, which we might miss if we went away with a too-simple notion of James's undoubted prescience.

One concerns the significance of the post-Durkheimian world itself. It means, as I said above, that our relation to the spiritual is being more and more unhooked from our relation to our political societies. But that by itself doesn't say anything about whether or how our relation to the sacred will be mediated by collective connections. A thoroughly post-Durkheimian society would be one in which our religious belonging would be unconnected to our national identity. It will almost certainly be one in which the gamut of such religious allegiances will be wide and varied. It will also almost certainly have lots of people who are following a religious life centered on personal experience in James's sense. But it doesn't follow that everyone, or even that most people, will be doing this. Many people will find their spiritual home in churches, for instance, including the Catholic church. In a post-Durkheimian world, this allegiance will be unhooked from that to a sacralized society (paleo style) or some national identity (neo style); but it will still be a collective connection.

These connections, sacramental or through a way of life, are obviously still powerful in the modern world. We have to avoid an easy error here—that of confusing the new place of religion in our personal and social lives, the framework understanding that we should be following our own spiritual sense, from the issue of what paths we will follow. The new framework has a strongly individualist component, but this will not necessarily mean that the content will be individuating. Many people will find themselves joining extremely powerful religious communities, because that's where many people's sense of the spiritual will lead them.

Of course, they won't necessarily sit easily in these communities as their forebears did. And in particular, a post-Durkheimian age may mean a much lower rate of intergenerational continuity of religious allegiance. But the strongly collective options will not lose adherents. Perhaps even the contrary trend might declare itself.

This is not to say that there is no connection between a post-Durkheimian dispensation, on one hand, and the tendency to an individualized experience of the spiritual that often slides toward the feel-good and the superficial. Clearly, this kind of undemanding spirituality is what a lot of people will understand as following their own way. Clearly, if one could in some way leap back to some earlier century, the number of self-indulgent seekers would radically decline. But all this is no excuse for repeating their mistake and just identifying the injunction to follow one's own spiritual path with the more flaccid and superficial options.

Some conservative souls feel that it is sufficient to condemn this age to note that it has led great numbers into modes of free-floating not very exigent spirituality. But they should ask themselves two questions: First, is it conceivable that one could return to a paleo- or even neo-Durkheimian dispensation? Second, and more profoundly, doesn't every dispensation have its own favored forms of deviation? If ours tends to multiply somewhat shallow and undemanding spiritual options, we shouldn't forget the spiritual costs of various kinds of forced conformity: hypocrisy, spiritual stultification, inner revolt against the Gospel, the confusion of faith and power, and even worse. Even if we had a choice, I'm not sure we wouldn't be wiser to stick with the present dispensation.

THE SECOND POINT that one might miss is the continuing importance of the neo-Durkheimian identities. In some societies these are in a quasi-agonistic relation to the post-Durkheimian climate. Think for instance of the United States, and certain demands of the Christian right, such as for school prayer. But these identities are perhaps even more in evidence among groups that feel suppressed or threatened (perhaps also the case of the Christian right?), and often people of a certain ethnic or historical identity will look to some religious marker to gather around. I have mentioned the Poles and Irish as examples. These were peoples cast into the modern political form because they were mobilized to attain their independence or establish their integrity in a context of being ruled from outside and sometimes being very heavily oppressed. They therefore took on the modern language and the modern conceptions of a political entity; they became in a modern sense peoples. And modern peoples, that is, collectivities that strive to be agents in history, need some understanding of what they're about, what I'm calling political identity. In the two cases mentioned, being Catholic was an important part of that identity.

This phenomenon remains important in the modern world, although from a faith perspective one might be ambivalent about it, because there is a gamut of cases, from a deeply felt religious allegiance all the way to situations in which the religious marker is cynically manipulated in order to mobilize people. Think of Milosević and of India's BJP. But whatever one's ethical judgments, this is a powerful reality in today's world, and one that is not about to disappear.

THE THIRD IMPORTANT THING that James seems to underrate is the way in which our response to our original spiritual intuitions may continue into formal spiritual practices. Here's where the foregrounding of feeling, and the moment of conversion and inspiration, take him away from the kind of religious life that may start in a moment of blinding insight, but then continues through some, perhaps very demanding spiritual discipline. It can take the form of meditation; it can take the form of prayer. One develops a religious life. Arguably this kind of path is becoming more and more prominent and widespread in our (largely) post-Durkheimian age. Many people are not satisfied with a momentary sense of wow! They want to take it further, and they're looking for ways of doing so.[1]

JAMES DIDN'T SEE ALL THIS. But this is hardly a reproach. How could anyone have? What is remarkable is that he saw so deeply into an essential feature of our divided age. In some sense religious "experience," the beginning intimations and intuitions that we feel bound to follow up, is crucial as never before, wherever we end up taking them in our divergent spiritual lives. It is because he saw this with such intensity, and could articulate it with such force, that James's book lives on so strongly in our world.

NOTES

NOTES

1. JAMES: *VARIETIES*

1. William James, *The Varieties of Religious Experience* (Harmondsworth: Penguin, 1982). Page references are to this edition.

2. Robert Tombs, *France: 1814–1914* (London: Longman, 1996), p. 135, places the high-water mark at 1880; Gérald Cholvy and Yves-Marie Hillaire, *Histoire religieuse de la France contemporaine: 1800/1880* (Paris: Privat, 1985), p. 317, set it earlier, around 1860. I have split the difference.

3. See John McManners, ed., *The Oxford History of Christianity* (Oxford: Oxford University Press, 1993), pp. 277–278. Jean Delumeau also speaks of this double process: "Depuis le 18e siècle, christianisation et déchristianisation ont marché de pair: christianisation d'une minorité et déchristianisation de la majorité"; quoted in Cholvy and Hillaire, *Histoire religieuse*, p. 313.

4. See W. K. Clifford, *The Ethics of Belief and other Essays,* ed. Leslie Stephen and F. Pollock (London: Watts, 1947).

5. See Henri Bremond's monumental *Histoire littéraire du sentiment religieux en France* (Paris: Armand Colin, 1967), especially vol. 1.

6. Ibid., vol 4.

7. The way in which *shar'ia* compliance articulates with a strong, personal, committed religious life is well illustrated in the study discussed by Clifford Geertz in his "William James" lecture, published as "The Pinch of Destiny: Religion as Experience, Meaning, Identity, Power," in his recent collected essays *Available Light* (Princeton: Princeton University Press, 2000), especially pp. 179 ff. I have greatly benefited from Geertz's lecture in my discussion of James here.

8. Max Weber, *Wirtschaft und Gesellschaft* (Tübingen: Mohr, 1922), pp. 759, 762.

9. Thus Robert Wuthnow, in his *After Heaven: Spirituality in America since the 1950s* (Berkeley: University of California Press, 1998), in discussing the increasing reports people give of meeting angels, and other similar experiences in recent years, notes that these tend to correlate with a religious upbringing in which realities of this kind had a place. See his chap. 5, especially pp. 125–126.

10. My discussion here has been much helped by Nicholas Lash's critique of James in his *Easter in Ordinary* (Notre Dame, Ind.: University of Notre Dame Press, 1986).

2. THE "TWICE-BORN"

1. See, for instance, David Martin's discussion in "The Evangelical Upsurge and Its Political Implications," in

The Desecularization of the World: Resurgent Religion and World: Politics, ed. Peter L. Berger (Grand Rapids: Eerdmans, 1999), pp. 37–49, and also his *Tongues of Fire* (Oxford: Blackwell, 1990).

2. Marcel Gauchet, *Le désenchantement du monde* (Paris: Gallimard, 1985).

3. William James, *The Will to Believe, and Other Essays in Popular Philosophy* (Cambridge, Mass.: Harvard University Press, 1979). Page references to this edition in the text are preceded by WB.

4. But even this stronger claim may have some truth to it: "I confess that I do not see why the very existence of the invisible world may not depend on the personal response which any one of us may make to the religious appeal. God himself, in short, may draw vital strength and increase of very being from our fidelity" (WB 55).

5. "Non intratur in veritatem, nisi per charitatem"; Augustine, *Contra Faustum,* lib. 32, cap. 18.

6. *Pensées,* quoted in Martin Heidegger, *Sein und Zeit* (Tübingen: Max Niemyer Verlag, 1967), p. 139 n. 1.

7. Geertz expresses very convincingly this extraordinary power of James: "The radically individualistic, subjectivistic, 'brute perception' concept of religion and religiousness, which his location as heir to New England intuitionism and his own encounter with the pinch of destiny led him into, was complemented by the intense, marvellously observant, almost pathologically

sensitive attention to the shades and subtleties of thought and emotion they also led him into"; "The Pinch of Destiny: Religion as Experience, Meaning, Identity, Power," in *Available Light* (Princeton: Princeton University Press, 2000), p. 185.

3. RELIGION TODAY

1. Ernst Kantorowicz, *The King's Two Bodies* (Princeton: Princeton University Press, 1997).

2. See Robert Bellah, "Civil Religion in America," in *Beyond Belief: Essays on Religion in a Post-Traditional World* (New York: Harper & Row, 1970), chap. 9.

3. E.g., David Martin, *Tongues of Fire* (Oxford: Blackwell, 1990) and *A General Theory of Secularization* (Oxford: Blackwell, 1978).

4. Linda Colley, *Britons* (New Haven: Yale University Press, 1992).

5. The connection of Christianity with decency in England has been noted by David Martin, *Dilemmas of Contemporary Religion* (Oxford: Blackwell, 1978), p. 122.

6. On this trend in working-class communities, see Richard Hoggart, *The Uses of Literacy* (London: Chatto & Windus, 1957). On the trend in peasant communities, see Yves Lambert, *Dieu change en Bretagne* (Paris: Cerf, 1985).

7. See Charles Taylor, *The Malaise of Modernity* (Toronto: Anansi, 1991).

8. Quoted from Samuel Hynes, *The Edwardian Turn of Mind* (Princeton: Princeton University Press, 1968), p. 325.

9. Michel Winock, *Le siècle des intellectuels* (Paris: Seuil, 1997), chap. 17.

10. See Charles Taylor, "Modern Social Imaginaries," forthcoming.

11. See Danièle Hervieu-Léger, *La religion pour mémoire* (Paris: Cerf, 1993), chap. 3, esp. pp. 82 ff.

12. Émile Durkheim, *Les formes élémentaires de la vie religieuse,* 5th ed. (Paris: Presses Universitaires Françaises, 1968).

13. Jean-Louis Schlegel makes the point that the values which constantly emerge from studies of young people today are "droits de l'homme, tolérance, respect des convictions d'autrui, libertés, amitié, amour, solidarité, fraternité, justice, respect de la nature, intervention humanitaire"; *Esprit,* no. 233 (June 1997): 29. Sylvette Denèfle concurs for her sample of French unbelievers in *Sociologie de la sécularisation* (Paris: L'Harmattan, 1997), chap. 6. Tolerance is for them the key virtue (pp. 166 ff).

14. Michael Sandel, *Democracy's Discontent* (Cambridge, Mass.: Harvard University Press, 1996), pp. 209–210.

15. Winock, *Le siècle des intellectuels,* p. 582.
16. François Furet, *Le passé d'une illusion* (Paris: Gallimard, 1996), points out how remarkable the allegiance was, and the sense of belonging that sustained it.
17. The excellent book by José Casanova, *Public Religions in the Modern World* (Chicago: University of Chicago Press, 1994), shows how diverse our religious predicament is. If we ever came to live in a predicament totally defined by the post-Durkheimian understanding, there would probably be no further space for religion in the public sphere. Spiritual life would be entirely privatized, in keeping with the norms of a certain procedural liberalism that is very widespread today. But Casanova traces in fact a "deprivatization" of religion, that is, an attempt by churches and religious bodies to intervene again in the political life of their societies. Instances are the Christian right and the Catholic bishops' letters in the United States. It is unlikely (and also undesirable) that this kind of thing ever cease. But the situation in which these interventions take place is defined by the end of a uniform Durkheimian dispensation, and the growing acceptance among many people of a post-Durkheimian understanding.
18. Luc Ferry in his very interesting *L'homme-Dieu, ou le sens de la vie* (Paris: Grasset, 1996), chap. 1, picks up on this phenomenon under the title "le refus de l'Autorité." I

agree with much of what he says, but I think he overintellectualizes this reaction by relating it directly to Descartes, instead of seeing its expressivist roots.

19. Sir George Trevelyan, in a lecture at the Festival for Mind, Body and Spirit, quoted in Paul Heelas, *The New Age Movement* (Oxford: Blackwell, 1996), p. 21. The injunction, one might say, represents only a New Age outlook. But in this respect, the various New Age movements accentuate much more widely held attitudes, as Heelas argues in chap. 6. In 1978, for instance, a Gallup poll found that 80 percent of Americans agreed that "an individual should arrive at his or her own religious beliefs independent of any churches or synagogues"; Heelas, p. 164; also cited in Robert Bellah et al., *Habits of the Heart* (Berkeley: University of California Press, 1985), p. 228.

20. Lambert, *Dieu change en Bretagne,* p. 373.

21. Religious sociologists had already noticed that the high level of practice in certain regions of France was tied to living within the parish. Migration to the cities generally had a devastating effect. As Gabriel Le Bras put it, "Je suis convaincu que sur cent ruraux qui s'établissent à Paris, il y en a à peu près 90 qui, au sortir de la gare Montparnasse, cessent d'être des pratiquants"; quoted in Danièle Hervieu-Léger, *Vers un nouveau Christianisme?* (Paris: Seuil, 1986), p. 37.

22. Lambert, *Dieu change en Bretagne*, p. 373.
23. Ibid., pp. 385 ff.
24. See Steve Bruce, *Religion in the Modern World* (Oxford: Oxford University Press, 1996), pp. 33, 137 ff.; Denèfle, *Sociologie de la sécularisation*.
25. For instance, the *Gallup Political & Economic Index* 394 (June 1993) reports that in Britain 40 percent believe in "some sort of spirit or lifeforce," as opposed to 30 percent who have faith in a "personal God"; cited in Heelas, *New Age Movement*, p. 166.
26. The move of many Western societies into what I have been calling a "post-Durkheimian" dispensation has obviously facilitated their move toward "multiculturalism," at the same time as this has become a more urgent issue because of the increasing diversity of their populations. But multiculturalism has also produced strains, which are often exacerbated by the continuing hold of one or other "Durkheimian" understanding on important segments of the population. Christian conservatives are made edgy by rampant expressivism in the United States; and many French people find it hard to see their country as containing an important Muslim component, so long have they related to it as an essentially Catholic country, or one defined by the constitutive tension between Catholicism and "laïcité."

4. SO WAS JAMES RIGHT?

1. See the very interesting discussion in Robert Wuthnow, *After Heaven: Spirituality in America since the 1950s* (Berkeley: University of California Press, 1998), chap. 7, "The Practice of Spirituality."